BOTH

✝

AND

Understanding apparent contradictions in Christianity

Ross Cunningham

CHRISTIAN FOCUS

commendations

'The God whom we worship is incomparable, unique and therefore incomprehensible. It is not surprising then that when God reveals himself to us in events, in narrative, in metaphor, in human language and in person that there should be mystery and even apparent contradictions. In this fresh and accessible book, Ross Cunningham addresses these antinomies of Christian faith and experience with clarity and faithfulness to the witness of Scripture. What is particularly valuable is his use of visual imagery to highlight each area of tension. This is a primer in Christian theology and a valuable resource for both personal and group reflection.'

Trevor Morrow
Former Moderator of the Presbyterian Church in Ireland; Minister Emeritus, Lucan Presbyterian Church, Dublin

'I recently read a book by two well-known scholars who spoke about the Book of Revelation as 'imagination,' yet they also spoke of it as a series of 'visions' from God. Was it a vision or was it the imagination? Yes, it was. That's an antinomy, two clashing ideas that are both true. Theology is filled with them, and they are both mysterious and beautifully liberating. God knows the human mind can't contain the fullness of truth, so God grants to us a series of 'both-ands'. The dearth of theology among so many is addressed in this short, snappy book that examines baskets of these tension points in our faith and it examines them fairly, clearly, and sensitively. What a wonderful idea for an introduction to Christian theology!'

Scot McKnight
Professor of New Testament, Northern Seminary, Lisle, Illinois

'As a minister in a multicultural, multi-language church, our people are ministering to many learning English, as well as partnering with a church for the deaf. I will be delighted to highlight this work to them. The combination of word and visual aid will help make difficult but essential Christian teachings more accessible to all. This book promotes a theology of balance, which is often lacking in our teaching today but is central to our Christian walk.'

Ivan Steen
Minister, Windsor Presbyterian Church, Belfast

'It is a primary responsibility of theologians from every generation to study well the orthodoxy of ages past and to translate it to the age in which she or he is located. This is what Ross has done with this introductory text on the perennial paradoxes of Christian faith. As a lay theologian, he writes with clarity and conciseness that renders accessible the complexity of doctrine without compromising on difficult truths. His lodestar is Scripture but he understands well the need to draw on the Church's thinking from two millennia, and he does so with remarkable balance and breadth. Christians from all traditions will benefit spiritually and practically from engaging with this book in personal reading and group study. I heartily commend it to you.'

Cynthia Bennett Brown
Lecturer in Systematic & Historical Theology, Belfast Bible College, Belfast

'*Both-And* is an insightful, creative, clarifying book that helps us think through the theological tensions that arise when we study the Bible. The illustrations and biblically grounded explanations memorably communicate these tensions so that we understand better both the complexity and simplicity of the big ideas of theology. I'm thankful for this excellent resource and expect that it will be of great help to those wanting to understand the answers to life's biggest questions.'

Erik Thoennes
Professor and Chair of Theology, Biola University; Pastor, Grace Evangelical Free Church of La Mirada, California

'In *Both-And* Ross Cunningham is taking the reader along the theological tracks he has walked, in order to show them the treasure he has found there. By wrestling with the rich and complex doctrines at the heart of the Christian Scriptures, and pressing into some of the apparent contradictions therein, he has discovered truth and beauty and goodness, which he shares in abundance in this book. This is a colourful and creatively presented introduction to profound theological truth that will stimulate both mind and heart.'

Reuben Hunter
Pastor, Trinity West Church, Shepherd's Bush, London

'In *Both-And* Ross Cunningham leads us with skilful poise on an exciting tightrope walk through twenty-three paradoxes of Christian theology and experience. He helps us find equilibrium in areas where sometimes we can very easily lose our balance. The author outlines a clear way forward, between apparent Christian ambiguities which many find confusing. Among the issues covered are: preservation and perseverance, blessings and curses, now and not yet, faith and reason, sorrow and joy, weakness and strength, confidence and humility, and love and obedience.'

Fergus Macdonald
Former Moderator of the Free Church of Scotland and General Secretary of the National Bible Society of Scotland

'Working with university students in a residential chaplaincy provides natural opportunities to journey with young people as they explore complex, and sometimes apparently contradictory, questions of faith and theology. This book is a fantastic platform to systematically explore the vital issues of belief for those who are keen to gain depth in their understanding. The book's creator visually connects and shapes our imagination and then skilfully addresses key concepts in his writing. It is a great teaching resource for small group settings, or an informal catalyst for conversations. I plan to harness its potential to help shape the thinking of a new generation of post-covid, young disciples of Jesus.'

David Gray
Presbyterian Chaplain, Queen's University, Belfast

'If you have ever felt that there are aspects of the Christian faith that are hard to hold together, this may be the book for you. How can God be both three and one, angry and loving, sovereign over everything, yet seeking human response? In the Christian life, can we be both weak and strong, free yet servants, in the world but not of it? Ross Cunningham's fresh and engaging exposition of Christian faith and life addresses such questions and many more, in a way that is both intellectually satisfying and pastorally helpful. The title *Both-And* conveys his essential insight: apparent contradictions in what Christianity affirms are not awkward embarrassments; rather they are woven into it, because God cannot be known in neat logical categories. The author's experience in the creative industries enables him to communicate deep things in concise, pithy, imaginative ways. I commend the book warmly.'

Gordon McConville
Emeritus Professor of Old Testament Theology, University of Gloucestershire, Cheltenham

'*Both-And* is clever, creative and clear. What a great way to learn theology! I loved the format, which avoids being gimmicky whilst, at the same time, clearly drawing attention to the truths it illustrates. Most Christians will benefit from reading Ross Cunningham's book—and a lot of non-Christians too. Taste and see...'

David Robertson
Author, Apologist, and Director of Third Space, City Bible Forum, Sydney

why this book?

AD 2020. It's hard to imagine anything new left to write about in the field of theology. We have the Bible, the Creeds, the Westminster Confession of Faith, and the writings of the many great minds who have helped defend and illuminate these truths across history (Augustine, Aquinas, Luther, Edwards, Spurgeon—to name but a few). Perhaps unsurprisingly then, you may find there is nothing new in this book. That, I hope, is a good thing—my intention is not to present any revised theology or radical re-interpretation of Scripture.

This reality, however, does raise the obvious question: if there's nothing new to say, then why write this book?

Having worked in the creative industry for over twenty years, I've often noticed that something new emerges when we bring together existing things in a different arrangement. In that sense, I believe there is something new to be found in this book—in the particular relationship between a series of apparent contradictions, a symbolic and reflective illustration style, and the consistent structural format of 'both-and'.

The positive outcome of this 'rearranging' process is that it often helps us rethink, or better capture, the essential truth of the existing content.

Another process I continue to practise in commercial design is 'reductionism'—the paring down of a solution to its simplest form, without losing its essence or modifying its truth. I felt this process could be faithfully applied to the apparent contradictions herein. In so doing, to help make the theological content more accessible to a broader range of learners.

We don't all learn in the same way—there are literary learners, visual learners, auditory learners and kinesthetic learners. With our lives now more interrupted than ever before, and our associated attention spans growing ever shorter, literary learning, in particular, is increasingly challenging.

My aim, therefore, was to create material with an emphasis on visual learning and reflection; and to present it in approachable bite-size chunks—as an alternative means of engagement for those who might, for various reasons, struggle to dive into a five-hundred-page tome on systematic theology.

'So why write this book?' In summary, because I believe God has been preparing me, through my profession, with the tools and passion to 'arrange something new that might widen the reach of something old'.

My prayer for the material is that essential theology will be introduced to a broader range of learners. And from that knowledge, that God's truth would be put into action in their lives—that they might become salt and light in the world.

Reading the Material

Although the chapters have been ordered by section, each has been written as a standalone piece. It is therefore not essential that the book is read in any particular order. The only thing I would recommend is to spend some time meditating on the illustrations and accompanying Bible verses before commencing each chapter.

Further Study

Included on the website www.bothand.org.uk is a downloadable study guide resource, which provides a framework to explore and discuss each chapter in more depth, within a small group setting.

introduction

Antinomy:
An apparent contradiction between conclusions which seem equally logical, reasonable or necessary.

Whether you're new to faith or have been a Christian all your life, you'll know that the Christian faith can often seem confusing. At times it even appears completely contradictory. The Bible reveals that Jesus is both fully God and fully man; that God is a being of mercy but also of wrath; that we are both saints and sinners in God's eyes—the list goes on. Lean too heavily towards either side of these apparently contradictory statements and, at worst, we fall into a world of heresy; at best, the simple life of faith becomes strained with misunderstanding and confusion.

This book presents twenty-three apparent contradictions in the Christian faith. Many could be classified as mere paradoxes and, with a little investigation, relatively quickly resolved. Other apparent contradictions, however, are not so straightforward. These are the great mysteries of the Bible. They are by their nature antinomies—appearing to be 'against themselves'—and often go beyond our realm of understanding. For example, it doesn't seem possible that the being of God could be three distinct persons, while each person is simultaneously fully God. Nor does it seem possible that Mary could bear a child, and at the same time be a virgin. Such mysteries require supernatural understanding in order to obtain a true sense of their meaning. Thankfully, God is at hand to help.

For the Lord gives wisdom; from his mouth come knowledge and understanding. (Prov. 2:6)

In every case of apparent contradiction, whether paradox or mystery, Scripture provides a clear framework to aid our understanding. The Bible doesn't try to reconcile both sides of the argument—it merely states both to be true. From this emerges a framework of 'both-and'. In other words, we are simply required to hold up both sides of these apparent contradictions as equally true and valid. Not to choose one over the other, but rather, to let them co-exist.

God has designed us with opposable thumbs so that we might apply two equal and opposite forces to get hold of physical objects. In the same way, we must learn to use two equal and opposite sides in our thinking to gain a deeper understanding of these great mysteries of our faith.

Charles Spurgeon, when asked how he could reconcile God's sovereignty with our human responsibility, replied simply: 'I never have to reconcile friends. Divine sovereignty and human responsibility have never had a falling out with each other. I do not need to reconcile what God has joined together.'

Adopting this mindset, our focus shifts from trying to resolve the mystery (which would be beyond our human limitations) to simply knowing how to recognise and treat it accordingly—to hold its apparently conflicting claims together.

My introduction to the concept of 'antimony' was from J.I. Packer's book, *Evangelism and the Sovereignty of God*. Packer begins by explaining that antinomies are not reserved for the world of Scripture. One of the best-known antinomies occurs in nature. In modern physics, light can be defined both as particles of energy (photons) and waves of energy (waveforms). Neither of these conclusions can be explained in terms of the other; however, both are equally true and valid. It is perhaps no coincidence this particular antinomy relates to the nature of light, a substance that God Himself is described as many times in the Bible. It points us to the reality that, in God, there is mystery far beyond the limits of our understanding.

This is the message we have heard from him and proclaim to you, that God is light, and in him is no darkness at all. (1 John 1:5)

Before getting into the main thrust of his argument, Packer provides the reader with an incredibly helpful framework for dealing with antinomies in general:

'What should one do, then, with an antinomy? Accept it for what it is and learn to live with it. Refuse to regard the apparent consistency as real; put down the semblance of contradiction to the deficiency of your own understanding; think of the two principles as not rival alternatives but, in some way that at present you do not grasp, complementary to each other … Note what connections exist between the two truths and their two frames of reference, and teach yourself to think of reality in a way that provides for their peaceful co-existence, remembering that reality itself has proved actually to contain them both. This is how antinomies must be handled, whether in nature or in Scripture. This, as I understand it, is how modern physics deals with the problem of light, and this is how Christians have to deal with the antinomies of biblical teaching.'

It is worth noting that Packer's entire book is devoted to the exploration of just one particular antinomy—the apparent contradiction between God's sovereignty and our human responsibility—and that topic itself is handled solely within the remit of evangelism. The significantly shorter texts in this book are not intended to provide a similarly comprehensive analysis. Instead, the aim is primarily to provide biblical verification that both sides of each apparent contradiction are true. We have a natural tendency to choose one side over the other—even though the Bible itself never actually does this. The texts explore the danger of this 'either-or' mentality and point us instead to the benefits of adopting a 'both-and' logic.

The illustrations at the start of each chapter are essential points to pause and reflect. They are designed to act as a visual memory aid to help balance both sides of the argument—to re-centre our thinking when we stray too far in either direction. By trusting the corresponding Bible verses that both sides of each apparent contradiction are true—the left page and the right page—we can begin to fix our thoughts on two seemingly opposite realities at the same time.

As mathematician and theologian Blaise Pascal commented: 'One shows one's greatness not by being at an extremity but by being simultaneously at two extremities and filling all the space between.'

Across the twenty-three chapters, this balanced mode of thinking will help us to know God more intimately; to better understand His amazing salvation for us; and, to live at peace in the world.

BOTH+AND
www.bothand.org.uk

1 Apparent contradictions in the divine nature.

2 Apparent contradictions in the experience of salvation.

3 Apparent contradictions in the characteristics of being in Christ.

1

Apparent contradictions in the divine nature.

three + one
God + man
holy + intimate
angry + merciful
general + specific

three

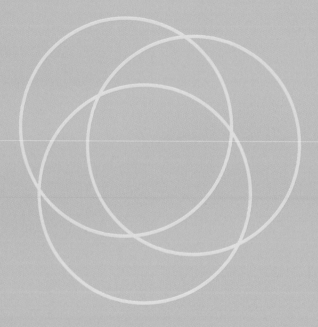

And when Jesus was baptised, immediately he went up
from the water, and behold, the heavens were opened to him,
and he saw the Spirit of God descending like a dove and
coming to rest on him; and behold, a voice from heaven said,
'This is my beloved Son, with whom I am well pleased.'

Matthew 3:16-17

one

Deuteronomy 6:4-5

'Hear, O Israel: The LORD our God, the LORD is one. You shall love the LORD your God with all your heart and with all your soul and with all your might.'

three + one

If you were to pause for a moment and pray to God, to whom would you instinctively direct your prayers? Would your intended recipient be God the Father, God the Son, or God the Holy Spirit—or maybe some broader sense of all three? The question is not designed to catch anyone out, but rather to demonstrate the inherent difficulty we have in grasping the fullness of the one true God. There are no divisions in God, and yet we understand Him in three distinct persons.

A.W. Tozer explains how God's being remains at one with Himself: 'The harmony of His being is the result not of a perfect balance of parts but of the absence of parts. Between His attributes no contradiction can exist. He need not suspend one to exercise another, for in Him all His attributes are one. All of God does all that God does; He does not divide Himself to perform a work, but works in the total unity of His being.'

In that sense, all three persons of God are fully present in everything God does, despite each person having a unique role in each event. This seemingly impossible relationship is established from Scripture (and later clarified in the Apostles' and Nicene Creeds) because it captures what the Apostles witnessed first-hand through the life of Jesus and by the illumination of the Spirit.

From these sources, we have discovered the doctrine of the Trinity, which faithfully presents the following three conclusions about God:

1. Father, Son and Holy Spirit are three distinct persons.
2. Each person is fully God.
3. There is only one God.

Combining these truths raises the obvious question: how is it possible that God can be both three and one at the same time? How can there be no division in God when He is revealed to us in three distinct persons?

To help us apprehend something of this great mystery, we first need to establish that God isn't three in the same way that He's one. God is one in essence, but three in person; and person and essence are not the same thing. As theologian Norman Geisler explained it: 'while essence is what you are, person is who you are'. So God could, therefore, be seen as one 'what' consisting of three 'who's'. In other words, God's singular divine essence is expressed in a dynamic relationship between three persons.

We can't pretend there isn't still a great mystery in this revelation—not least because we have no other context for such a being. For that reason, any analogy we might use to explain the Trinity falls short of adequately describing the incredible reality. Even though the term 'trinity' doesn't appear in Scripture, the reality of 'tri-unity'—of threeness in oneness—is present in the Bible from start to finish. That God is one is a foundational Old Testament confession:

'Hear, O Israel: The Lord our God, the Lord is one. You shall love the Lord your God with all your heart and with all your soul and with all your might.' (Deut. 6:4-5)

Because He is Creator of all that is, heaven, earth and sea (Gen. 1:1), and because He rescued the Israelites from their sin, the covenant God is Lord, and there is no other like Him:

Therefore you are great, O Lord God. For there is none like you, and there is no God besides you, according to all that we have heard with our ears. (2 Sam. 7:22)

Only one being can be fully in control of all other beings such that they have this level of authority, or exercise this sort of control. God is one. There is no other. However, this one God is also revealed in Scripture in three persons: the Father, the Son and the Holy Spirit; and while their deity is revealed most clearly in the New Testament, the seeds of this threeness are present from the beginning. When the one God creates, He does so by speaking His Word and sending His Spirit (Gen. 1:2).

In the beginning was the Word, and the Word was with God, and the Word was God. (John 1:1)

And the Word became flesh and dwelt among us, full of grace and truth; we have beheld his glory, glory as of the only Son from the Father. (John 1:14)

John's gospel account of creation establishes the remarkable truth that Jesus was the Word; the same Word who was not only with God in the beginning but also 'was' God. The Holy Spirit is also revealed to be God in several passages of Scripture:

No one comprehends the thoughts of God except the Spirit of God. (1 Cor. 2:11)

'Ananias, why has Satan filled your heart to lie to the Holy Spirit? You have not lied to humans, but to God.' (Acts 5:3-4)

Combining the overall revelation of Scripture then, we are presented with the unlikely model of the triune God: God the Father, God the Son and God the Holy Spirit are all the one God, yet in three persons. We see this reality most clearly at

Jesus' baptism: Father, Son and Holy Spirit are all present in this earth-shaking scene as Jesus prepares for His earthly ministry.

And when Jesus was baptised, immediately he went up from the water, and behold, the heavens were opened to him, and he saw the Spirit of God descending like a dove and coming to rest on him; and behold, a voice from heaven said, 'This is my beloved Son, with whom I am well pleased.' (Matt. 3:16-17)

Biblical revelation, then, is unmistakably trinitarian, as all of God is present in all that He does.

God is one; God is three. A biblical perspective on such an awesome reality should lead us to the same conclusion as one of the ancient champions of trinitarian theology, Gregory Nazianzen, who put his experience like this: 'I cannot think on the one without quickly being encircled by the splendour of the three; nor can I discern the three without being straightway carried back to the one.'

This continuous moving back and forward, between two apparently contradictory truths, is precisely the model of thinking advocated throughout this book. To rest only on one truth, at the expense of the other, leads to an impoverished view of God. In history, wrong-thinking of this nature has led to many heresies. At one extreme, dropping God's oneness means that Father, Son and Spirit effectively become three separate Gods, leading to a form of polytheism. At the other extreme, dropping God's threeness results in the demotion of Jesus to a created human being, and the Holy Spirit to merely the tangible 'effect' of God.

Although such simplifications may seem less problematic to our finite intelligence, they are not what Scripture reveals, and serve only to destroy the gospel. They create hierarchies in the Godhead that make the events of the cross untenable. As we'll cover more fully in the next chapter, without Jesus' full divinity, both His sacrifice and our salvation would be incomplete. Furthermore, some of the most misguided conclusions about God have arisen from such wrong-thinking. Some scholars have even presented a terrible caricature of God as a brutal father, acting like some sort of cosmic child-abuser of His Son. Remembering both God's oneness and threeness safeguards us from such abominations. It also points us to a depth of love that resonates with our deepest desires. Within the Godhead is a depth of love that is shared with all who would receive it. As theologian James M. Houston puts it: 'the eternal character of God's love is that of love given, love received and love shared'.

In summary, God—this amazing dynamic relational being—chooses to call us into relationship with Him; that we might share in relationship with a being who is in perfect relationship. The Spirit then leads us into unity in the church. In so doing, the self-abandoning love of God overflows into the life of His people. We are then called as a body of believers to share this same love in the world. What a joy and a privilege to be connected to the source of all love!

God is one, and God is three—uniquely glorious in majesty—a dynamic relational God beyond our full comprehension, worthy of our wonder, love and praise.

God

Jesus said to them, 'Truly, truly, I say to you, before Abraham was, I AM.'

John 8:58

man

1 Timothy 2:5

For there is one God, and there is one mediator between God and men, the man Christ Jesus.

God + man

In the early church, there was almost no controversy around the claims of the deity of Christ. In the gospels, we see that Jesus claimed to be God and then backed His claim up with actions.

Jesus said: 'Truly, truly, I say to you; before Abraham was, I AM.' (John 8:58)

And [Jesus] awoke and rebuked the wind and said to the sea: 'Peace! Be still!' And the wind ceased, and there was a great calm. (Mark 4:39)

Taking [a dead girl] by the hand, he said to her 'Talitha cumi' which means 'little girl I say to you, arise.' And immediately the girl got up and began walking. (Mark 5:41-42)

John records Jesus using about Himself the covenant name of God ('I AM'), and then Mark recounts Him, amongst other things, commanding the creation and raising the dead; acting with divine authority. In Paul's letter to the Colossians, he affirms Jesus' deity as follows:

For in him the whole fullness of deity dwells bodily. (Col. 2:9)

Where the early church had problems was in accepting the humanity of Jesus. So impressed were they by His life and words, by His evident divinity, it seemed impossible that He was truly human. Many argued that Jesus only 'seemed' to be human. These people were called 'docetists' (from the Greek word 'dokeo', meaning 'to seem'). They believed that despite His body having the appearance of humanity, He was, in fact, a purely spiritual being.

Each of the gospels, however, tell a very different story. Again and again, these eyewitness accounts record Jesus experiencing emotions and actions that are exclusively human: He gets tired (Matt. 14:13), hungry (Mark 11:12), distressed (Luke 22:44), sad (John 11:35), and He experiences the pain of physical punishment. These are uniquely human, physical experiences. John leaves us in no doubt when he says:

And the Word became flesh and dwelt among us. (John 1:14)

The Word translated 'flesh' here has an earthy simplicity to it. John is using earthy language to describe a very physical reality. Jesus, just like Adam before Him, came to be a true man. Theologian John Frame comments: 'Like Adam and Adam's descendants, Jesus lived in a body that was made of dust, part of the creation. In that body, he lived, ate, drank, suffered, died, and was buried. In that body, he was raised from the dead.'

The fact of the incarnation is evident in the gospels, but what does it mean? In the early debates around the issue, the Council of Chalcedon (451 AD) explained it as a union of divine and human natures in one person:

'... one and the same Christ, Son, Lord, Only-begotten, recognised in two natures, without confusion, without change, without division, without separation: the distinction in natures being in no way annulled by the union, but rather the characteristics of each nature being preserved and coming together to form one person and subsistence, not as parted or separated into two persons, but one and the same Son and Only-begotten God the Word, Lord Jesus Christ...'

The second person of the Trinity comes to earth, taking to His divinity a human nature. In Jesus, humanity and divinity co-exist. Where God is one essence in three persons, Jesus Christ is one person with two natures.

So the Bible reveals Jesus as fully God and fully man—but what are the implications for us? Why is it important that Jesus was both infinite and finite, invisible and visible, eternal and temporal, all-knowing and yet, as we read in Matthew 24:36, appears unsure about the future? The answer is because, without both natures, our salvation would otherwise be void. When we consider God's wider plan of salvation for humanity, we see clear biblical evidence that in order for Jesus' sacrifice to be effective, He had to have both natures present at the cross. His human nature was necessary so that He could be like the people He would redeem:

But when the fullness of time had come, God sent forth his Son, born of a woman, born under the law, to redeem those who were under the law, so that we might receive adoption as sons. (Gal. 4:4-5)

Therefore he had to be made like his brothers in every respect, so that he might become a merciful and faithful high priest in the service of God, to make propitiation for the sins of the people. (Heb. 2:17)

While on earth, Jesus chose to limit Himself (concerning certain divine attributes) in order to redeem a sinful humanity and restore our broken cosmos. Just as Adam, the man, plunged the earth into chaos, so it took Jesus Christ, the man, to bring restoration and redemption. In His earthly ministry, Jesus demonstrated that He had access to His Father's power (Matt. 26:51-54), and was ministering entirely as a man under the law (Gal. 4:4-5), doing miracles by the power of the Holy Spirit.

He embraced self-limitation and became completely human, completely dependent upon God in order to be a perfect sacrifice for sin. So Jesus' humanity is essential to our salvation.

But what about His divinity? Why did He also need to be the God-man? The New City Catechism puts it like this:

'That because of his divine nature his obedience and suffering would be perfect and effective; and also that he would be able to bear the righteous anger of God against sin and yet overcome death.'

Clearly, the accomplishment of salvation could not be borne by someone merely human. Something beyond our human limitations was required in order to be able to bear the wrath of God. Thus Jesus' divine nature was also critical to the effectiveness of His sacrifice.

God raised him up, loosing the pangs of death, because it was not possible for him to be held by it. (Acts 2:24)

In conclusion, the Bible explains how our restoration depends on this glorious truth that Jesus was both fully man and fully God. He needed to be fully man to stand in our place as an appropriate sacrifice for humanity; He needed to be fully God to do the impossible and triumph over death. Furthermore, it's not just our restoration that required the God-man—all aspects of God's redemptive plan required this incredible duality of nature.

Jonathan Edwards summarises the following achievements in God's great work of redemption: conquering evil (1 John 3:8); restoring the world (Isa. 65:17); uniting all things (Eph. 1:11); beautifying the elect (Eph. 5:14); and, glorifying the Godhead (John 13:31-32). All this through His incredible atoning sacrifice on the cross.

Jesus, the God-man—our perfect redeemer—making all things new and bringing glory to God in the highest.

holy

'For my thoughts are not your thoughts, neither are your
ways my ways' declares the LORD. 'For as the heavens
are higher than the earth, so are my ways higher than
your ways and my thoughts than your thoughts.'

Isaiah 55:8-9

intimate

Luke 12:6-7

'Are not five sparrows sold for two pennies? And not one of them is forgotten before God. Why, even the hairs of your head are all numbered. Fear not; you are of more value than many sparrows.'

holy + intimate

What is the one characteristic of God for which you are most thankful? Is it His goodness, His mercy, or maybe His love? Is it likely that anyone would choose His holiness? Probably not; and yet, holiness is arguably the single most important attribute of God. R.C. Sproul comments that only one attribute of God is ever elevated to the third degree, citing the refrain 'holy, holy, holy' found in Isaiah 6:3 and Revelation 4:8.

If we were to hear someone described as 'holy', it would most likely be on account of their high standard or frequency of religious activity. However, the virtue being described in such a case is 'piety', rather than 'holiness'. Piety and holiness are not the same.

To be holy means to be set apart. Holiness comes from the idea of separation—of being cut off. A reasonable analogy might be to imagine preparing a pineapple for eating. When a knife is used to cut and separate the edible fruit from the prickly husk and crown, it effectively sets apart the best material. The off-cuts go to the bin, while the good material is set apart with a higher purpose and value. That's the idea of being holy: to be set apart and of higher value. It's God's holiness, this being set apart from us, that makes Him so different to us. He's not like us. In fact, God is significantly more 'not' like us than He is like us. It is true that humanity was made in the image of God (Gen. 1:26); however, it is easy to read this and overemphasise our sameness. In reality, this verse has more to do with the curatorial authority God granted us over creation (and the faculties thereby required), rather than our particular similarities. As many have postulated, it would probably be fair to assume we have more in common with our household pet than we do with an infinitely holy God—the God who created the heavens and earth out of nothing:

'Where were you when I laid the foundation of the earth? Tell me, if you have understanding.'
(Job 38:4)

This gulf in holiness is why the full glory of God's presence is too much for a fallen humanity to bear. Even as Christians, until Jesus (the author and finisher of our faith) returns to complete our glorification, we aren't holy enough to stand in the presence of the one true God.

'… you cannot see my face, for no one may see me and live.' (Exod. 33:20)

For this reason, we see God appearing in Scripture in what are called theophanies (where He takes on other forms to prevent fatal encounters). He appears at different critical points in our history as a man, an angel, a pillar of cloud or fire. Even Moses did not receive the privilege of looking upon God's face. This vast chasm between God and us should give us a keen sense of the appropriate response to a being of such infinite power. When Isaiah sees a vision of the Lord, his trembling response is to see, by sharp contrast, his own frailties and those of his people:

And I said: 'Woe is me! For I am lost; for I am a man of unclean lips, and I dwell in the midst of a people of unclean lips; for my eyes have seen the King, the LORD of hosts!' (Isa. 6:5)

This coming undone in response to God's holiness is often misrepresented as a negative, fearful response. We might ask: how can we fear someone whom we should also love? However, fear in the Hebrew language is a more nuanced concept than we might imagine. The Bible explains that the fear of the Lord is the beginning of wisdom (Prov. 9:10). There are two Hebrew words for fear: 'yirah' and 'pachad'. Genuine fear or panic, outside of the context of God, is always treated by the Hebrew word 'pachad'. This would be more akin to how we interpret the word fear in our language today, perhaps similar to what people mean when they talk about the 'fight or flight' response—something of a mindless panic. 'Yirah' fear, however, is always used in response to God and often means something more like awe in our language. Abraham Heschel describes the full meaning of yirah:

'According to the Bible the principle religious virtue is yirah. What is the nature of yirah? The word has two meanings, fear and awe. There is the man who fears the Lord lest he be punished in his body, family, or in his possessions. Another man fears the Lord because he is afraid of punishment in the life to come … Awe, unlike fear, does not make us shrink from the awe-inspiring object, but, on the contrary, draws us near to it. This is why awe is comparable to both love and joy ... In a sense, awe is the antithesis of fear.'

Awe holds us in that climactic tension where we can both fear and love the Lord at the same time. God's holiness, His complete otherness, His separation from the sin we know in ourselves, is what generates fear and trembling. Nevertheless, because He is love, expressed in the death of His Son, we are drawn to Him despite the chasm between us.

For I, the LORD your God, hold your right hand; it is I who say to you, 'Fear not, I am the one who helps you.' (Isa. 41:13)

Not only is God the holy one, heard in the roar of mighty thunder; He is also to be found in the still small voice—the intimate whisper that leads us through the peaks and valleys.

For you formed my inward parts; you knitted me together in my mother's womb. I praise you, for I am fearfully and wonderfully made... [or, fearfully set apart]. (Ps. 139:13-14)

He knows our innermost thoughts and workings and cares for our every detail in our lives.

'Are not five sparrows sold for two pennies? And not one of them is forgotten before God. Why, even the hairs of your head are all numbered. Fear not; you are of more value than many sparrows.' (Luke 12:6-7)

Though He is boundless in power and limitless beyond our imagination (Job 38), He nevertheless directs His goodness towards every atom and molecule of His vast creation. As His people, we receive His special affection and care.

Without this counter-balance of intimacy to God's holiness, where the veil of heaven is drawn back, and God touches human hearts individually, there would remain only fear. We know this is no recipe for a loving relationship. God, however, draws near to us. He makes Himself familiar and allows us to know Him on several levels: through nature (Rom. 1:18-20); through His Word (2 Tim. 3:16); especially through His Son (John 1:18), whose revelation is in the Word; and ultimately through the work of the Holy Spirit (1 Cor. 12:3), who draws us to Christ so that we may be reconciled to God. This movement of God to reach out to us in love demonstrates His surprising grace. Moreover, if He did not make the first move—if He did not first love us—He would remain unreachable.

In summary, without God's intimate fatherly care, He would be impossible to love. Without His infinite holiness, He wouldn't be worth loving. He would be too similar to us—not majestic enough to be held in the kind of awe that leads us to fall on our knees in wonder, love and praise.

angry

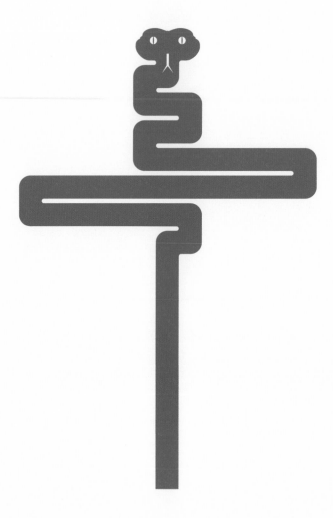

For our sake he made him to be sin who knew no sin, so that in him we might become the righteousness of God.

2 Corinthians 5:21

merciful

John 3:14-15

'Just as Moses lifted up the serpent in the wilderness,
so must the Son of Man be lifted up, that whosoever
believes in him may have eternal life.'

angry + merciful

Perhaps you've heard the statement: 'God hates the sin, but loves the sinner'? Maybe you've even found some comfort in this notion... but is it true? Consider what the Bible says about this:

For you are not a God who delights in wickedness; evil may not dwell with you. The boastful shall not stand before your eyes; you hate all evildoers. You destroy those who speak lies; the LORD abhors the bloodthirsty and deceitful man. (Ps. 5:4-6)

Harsh as it sounds, we can't sugar-coat the reality that God is angry at 'us'. Ironically, to play down His righteous anger only serves to minimise His grace in the process. We need to remember that God's mercy is offered to us while we are still at enmity with Him. He has every right to be angry at us; and yet He forgives us and offers grace and mercy, despite our repeated tendency to turn our backs on Him. Lest we confuse God's righteous anger here with our fallen (and often grotesquely twisted) human anger, we should note the difference quickly. God's anger arises from a heart that is grieved by sin:

And the LORD was sorry that he had made man on the earth, and it grieved him to his heart. (Gen. 6:6)

His wrath is, therefore, a natural response to the human condition. Scripture helps make clear why God, to this day, still has a right to be angered at us personally. It explains that each one of us is born into sin (Rom. 3:23) and that God is angry at both sin and sinner alike (John 3:36). With those truths in mind, it raises the obvious question: if we are all, as the title of Jonathan Edwards' famous sermon suggests, 'Sinners in the hands of an angry God', how is it fair for some to receive God's mercy and others to receive His wrath? Shouldn't we all be cast equally in condemnation—or, the reverse—if God truly loves us, shouldn't we all receive His mercy, irrespective of our shortcomings? The Bible, however, is clear that some will receive mercy, and others will receive wrath (Rom. 9:22-23). This process, however little we may understand God's motives, cannot be viewed as either arbitrary or unfair. Deuteronomy 32:4 states that God is just in all His ways. Since God is also the very definition of love (1 John 4:8), we can only conclude that there must be perfect justice and love manifest in His judgement of humanity.

Understanding how God can rightly display both mercy and anger in His treatment of humanity points us to the very core idea of the gospel—that Jesus stood in our place to take the wrath of God for us. Under His protection, we receive mercy instead of wrath. This exchange is only made possible through 'substitutionary atonement'. Jesus was the substitute, sacrificed in our place to atone for our sin. Notice how it works: God's righteous anger at all the sin and brokenness in the world does not magically evaporate into the heavens. Instead, it is pointed at a substitute: Jesus—God in flesh. He stands in our place and takes the penalty of sin that we deserve. Covered by His actions, we receive His undeserved forgiveness and mercy instead.

The Bible helpfully gives us several ways to understand this great exchange of mercy for wrath (historical, covenantal, familial, judicial, etc.) The theme of Passover is particularly strong throughout Scripture, connecting a thread from the first blood sacrifices of the Israelites, right through to Jesus' crucifixion. In the story of the Passover (Exod. 12), the Israelites marked their door-posts with the blood of a lamb which spared them from God's wrath. This concept prepares us for the identification of Jesus as the 'lamb of God' in John 1:29. At the last supper, Jesus explains that the wine represents His blood, shed on the cross, forever replacing the requirement for further sacrifice. So Jesus became the ultimate 'scapegoat'—the ransom paid for the sins of the world (Matt. 20:28). Thus by repenting from our sinful state and sharing in His death, Jesus' blood spares us from our due penalty.

We often try to separate God's anger from His mercy by making a corresponding division between the Old and New Testament. The misconception is that the Old Testament God is full of anger, whereas, in the New Testament, Jesus comes (as the Son of God) full of love and mercy. However, right from the beginning of the Bible, we see both mercy and anger co-existing. After the flood, in Genesis 9, God extends His everlasting covenant promise with Noah. On sealing this promise, He gives us the sign of the rainbow to remind us that all of creation will be protected from His wrath. Commentators on this passage note that the translation of 'rainbow' here is actually 'warrior-bow', stressing that the bow is pointing back to heaven. This sign reminds us that God's anger at us is not 'waived'. It is pointed back at Himself. God, in the person of Jesus, takes the wrath; and, through repentance, we receive His forgiveness and mercy. Amazing grace.

In another fascinating Old Testament account, in Numbers 21:4-9, we witness the Israelites being attacked by snakes in the wilderness. The people were grumbling and had grown openly rebellious against God. In righteous anger at their sin, God sends in a den of venomous snakes to act as a judgement. On the surface, it seems like harsh treatment. However, viewed from an eternal perspective, it reads as a merciful act since it serves to wake the Israelites up to the impending eternal death of their wayward souls. Moses then intercedes for his people and is instructed by God to put a bronze serpent on a staff and raise it for all to see. Anyone who looked up to the bronze serpent would be saved from the attacking snakes. The bronze serpent represented God's judgement of the people. There was a weighing of the heart initiated through this judgement, and a personal response was required. Would the people put their trust in the Lord, and look to the authority and salvation of God behind the lifted serpent?

The story has a simple yet uncompromising narrative. Mercy is found by those who trust God to deliver them from His righteous anger at their wrong-doing. The story finds its parallel in the New Testament, where Jesus surprisingly likens Himself directly to this bronze serpent:

'Just as Moses lifted up the serpent in the wilderness, so must the Son of Man be lifted up, that whosoever believes in him may have eternal life.' (John 3:14-15)

So Jesus said to them, 'When you have lifted up the Son of Man, then you will know that I am he, and that I do nothing on my own authority, but speak just as the Father taught me.' (John 8:28)

So on the cross, we see Jesus lifted up as the ultimate judgement. The same question is asked of us today through this judgement: will we repent and put our trust in the Lord's mercy, accepting the authority and salvation of God behind the lifted-up Christ? Will we take refuge in Christ and shield ourselves from God's righteous anger? Jesus came to stand in our place and receive the wrath we deserve. If we look to Him, to the authority of God behind the lifted-up Christ, we are freed from condemnation and receive the riches of His mercy. On the cross, Jesus received the wrath of God against sin. The Bible reveals the incredible truth that Jesus became sin, in order that the wrath of God might bury sin once and for all. As Paul explains:

For our sake he made him to be sin who knew no sin, so that in him we might become the righteousness of God. (2 Cor. 5:21)

This is the good news: we are not just shielded by Christ, we are counted righteous in Him. Nevertheless, even though mercy triumphs over wrath for those who are counted righteous in Christ, it remains vital in our Christian practice not to forget the present reality of both God's mercy and His anger. Minimising either reality cheapens God's grace and calls His justice into question.

If we play down God's anger, we immediately neglect the gravity with which God views sin. Consider what it cost God to offer us His mercy. God's anger was pointed at Himself, even to death on a cross. His justice needed to be served. If His anger had instead been simply waived, with no substitution to take His wrath, then His justice would be called into question. Other religions often circumvent this need for higher justice with gods who can cancel debts at no cost, with no ensuing wrath.

Such deities may be merciful, but cannot be entirely just at the same time. The God of the Bible is without injustice (Deut. 32:4). His righteous anger is a critical component of His justice.

On the other hand, if we neglect God's mercy, we end up with a predominantly angry God. It inevitably results in a tireless effort to appease Him and thus avoid His anger. In this case, we imagine our personal record and good works somehow determine God's level of favour on us. There is no security in this state—it is not a state of grace. By the grace of God, salvation comes from Christ alone (Eph. 2:8). Our good works are not unimportant of course—they are appointed by God for us to fulfil—but our fulfilment of them is merely a sign that we are saved, rather than a means to becoming saved.

Salvation comes from the Lord. His mercy triumphs. We are a forgiven people; shielded from His righteous anger by Christ's work alone. Thanks be to God.

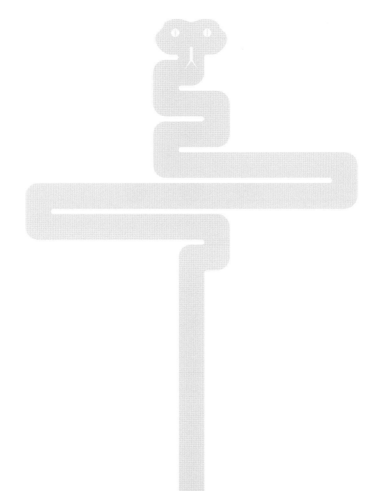

general

[God] makes his sun rise on the evil and on the good,
and sends rain on the just and on the unjust.

Matthew 5:45

specific

Ephesians 2:8

For by grace you have been saved through faith. And this is not your own doing; it is the gift of God.

general + specific

When the Bible speaks about God's grace, it presents two clear categories. Firstly, God's common grace—His general goodness to all of creation; and secondly, God's saving grace—His specific mercy and goodness to redeem His elect people.

You may be wondering where the contradiction appears in these two modes of grace. In reality, there isn't one. However, we know by experience that, as Christians, we often tend to be more focused on God's specific 'saving grace' to His elect, rather than His more general 'common grace' to all of creation. With such an emphasis, we might wrongly imagine that God is indifferent to the lost, while the thrust of His goodness is towards His elect people. The Bible, however, presents a more nuanced picture of grace. It is both general and specific. And if we aren't keenly aware of both states of grace, our ability to make sense of the gospel to the world around us is harmfully eroded.

It has often been said that our view of humanity determines our view of salvation. The more we see our hopelessness with clarity, the more grateful we become for God's saving grace. Understanding the doctrine of common grace leads us to a correct understanding of the hopelessness of the human condition—that the heart is 'deceitful above all things, and desperately sick' (Jer. 17:9). Consequently, part of the operation of God's common grace is actually to restrain this natural tendency towards evil in humanity. Many of us, Christians included, don't like to hear this. We tend to assume that humanity is inherently good, or at least has the capacity to choose good or evil, irrespective of God's influence. However, this is not the reality presented by the Bible. Even those outside of God, who appear to be 'good' people, are only able to function this way in society because God restrains their capacity for evil. This is why John the Baptist and Jesus always presented a gospel of repentance—because God's saving grace is the only hope to turn to for a humanity that, outside of God's common grace, would be even more rapidly bound for depravity and destruction.

God's common grace is revealed to humanity in three particular ways:

1. God is good and merciful to all people.

The Lord is good to all, and his mercy is over all that he has made. (Ps. 145:9)

This gift from the Lord is freely received in much of what we experience in life—sun, rain, nature, food, air, breath, movement, relationships, even our work. As Paul explains:

... for he did good by giving you rains from heaven and fruitful seasons, satisfying your hearts with food and gladness. (Acts 14:17)

Matthew's gospel account stresses that such favour is for all—not just the elect:

For he makes his sun rise on the evil and on the good, and sends rain on the just and on the unjust. (Matt. 5:45)

2. God grants the ability to all people to perform works of goodness and creativity which benefit society.

Each one of us, elect or not, has the knowledge of the law of God placed in our hearts. This moral compass that God graces our fallen humanity with, enables everyone to perform acts of goodness in society:

For when Gentiles, who do not have the law, by nature do what the law requires, they are a law to themselves, even though they do not have the law. They show that the work of the law is written on their hearts... (Rom. 2:14-15)

We are also inherently gifted with creative ability. In all walks of life, we see incredible feats of creative talent. Often, such work—made possible by God's common grace—is pregnant with divine truth and meaning. Much that would appear to be secular on the surface, is brimming with the potential for divine revelation. When Paul preaches to the Greeks in the Areopagus (Acts 17:22-34), he explains that their statue 'to an unknown God' represents the Creator of the universe—the God who cannot be carved in stone. Paul makes reference to a Greek poet called Aratus, quoting a line from a well-known poem: 'In him we live and move and have our being'. Although Aratus was referring to Zeus, Paul claims this truth for the God who is, as yet, unknown to them.

In general, truths about God can be found in all sorts of secular creative human endeavour—especially in the arts. Sometimes this is intentional, as in C.S. Lewis's *Narnia* or J.R.R. Tolkien's *Lord of the Rings*, in other cases it is latent, picking up on our Spirit-shaped longing for the divine. Even in writing that appears to promote atheism or attack Christianity (Philip Pullman's *His Dark Materials* for example), there remains a sense of spirituality and a belief in the possibility of things beyond our comprehension. God, in His wisdom and mercy, may even use such narratives to bring His children from darkness into the light. Phil Togwell, speaking on the Lectio 365 devotional, describes how he was 'set free' from a dark period in his life, by truth that God spoke to him through a song he heard in a pub in north London.

3. God restrains sin in the life of the individual and society.

... the LORD said to him, 'Not so! If anyone kills Cain, vengeance shall be taken on him sevenfold.' And the LORD put a mark on Cain, lest any who found him should attack him. (Gen. 4:15)

Immediately after the fall of humanity, we witness God restraining evil, as Cain is protected from harmful intent. Later in the book of Genesis, God restrains Abimelech from touching Abraham's wife Sarah:

Then God said to him in the dream, 'Yes, I know that you have done this in the integrity of your heart, and it was I who kept you from sinning against me. Therefore I did not let you touch her.' (Gen. 20:6)

That God would purposefully restrain our sin leads us to the 'doctrine of total depravity'. As mentioned, this doctrine is not liked by many—partly because we often have too high a view of humanity; and partly because the doctrine is often misunderstood. 'Total depravity' does not mean that someone is as evil as they could possibly be, or is without any conscience or moral compass. Rather, the doctrine of total depravity teaches that as a result of the fall of humanity (Gen. 3:6) every part of a person—body, mind, will and emotions—has been corrupted in some way by sin. In other words, 'total' refers to the full 'reach' of depravity across each person's faculties, rather than the 'extent' of an individual's depravity. Every part of everyone is at least touched and tainted to some degree by sin. As a result, all our thoughts and deeds are seen as filthy rags before the Lord (Isa. 64:6).

Ironically, if God's common grace did not restrain our sinful actions, we would eventually experience a scenario more akin to what many confuse the term 'total depravity' to mean—total unrestrained evil. The situation in Noah's day possibly gives us a foretaste of this condition:

The LORD saw that the wickedness of man was great in the earth, and that every intention of the thoughts of his heart was only evil continually. (Gen. 6:5)

If humanity is left without God's common grace for long enough, our condition could easily be imagined as hell—of pure rebellion against God, playing out eternally. In hell, God's common grace is gone—none of the previously mentioned blessings (sun, rain, nature, food, air, breath, movement, relationships, work) would be bestowed on hell's inhabitants. The picture C.S. Lewis paints of hell is that of a soul so dehumanised that it constitutes only of its sin—of an angry grumbling mood persisting eternally. Nothing is left in hell except that which is in rebellion to God. If this is true, it concurs with certain details of the story of the rich man in hell (Luke 16), who's so dehumanised that he's not even given a name. The absence of God's common grace in hell also helps address one of the big elephants in the room—how do we accept God's justice if our closest loved ones are judged worthy of hell?

In this dreadful scenario, we must remember that all the potential for good in those relationships with our loved ones was only ever possible by God's common grace. In hell, all those good things would be removed. To that end, the memories we might have of a loving mother, or beautiful daughter would be of characteristics that would be totally lost in hell. We could assume, were we to visit hell, that we would in no way recognise our loved ones there. For what we loved in them would be lost.

Of course, while this understanding may 'de-personalise' the notion of torment to an extent, it certainly doesn't resolve the great sadness of a lost soul. If anything, it should underline the hopelessness of our human condition—and our desperate need for a saviour.

Praise be to the God and Father of our Lord Jesus Christ, who opens the eyes of our hearts to recognise our spiritual state. God's saving grace gives us faith in Christ to turn our hopeless condition into a triumph of immeasurable riches:

[We] were by nature children of wrath, like the rest of mankind. But God, being rich in mercy, because of the great love with which he loved us, even when we were dead in our trespasses, made us alive together with Christ—by grace you have been saved—and raised us up with him and seated us with him in the heavenly places in Christ Jesus, so that in the coming ages he might show the immeasurable riches of his grace in kindness towards us in Christ Jesus. (Eph. 2:3-7)

In summary, it is vital to remember that God's grace is both general and specific. Contemplating the absence of God's common grace—the total depravity of humanity—leads us to the inevitable conclusion that we *all* desperately need His saving grace.

Praise God that by His mercy, not only is our evil is restrained but, through Christ, complete restoration is made possible.

2

Apparent contradictions in the experience of salvation.

universal + elective

master + messenger

perseverance + preservation

decided + unfolding

death + life

blessings + curses

now + not yet

natural + supernatural

personal + public

faith + reason

universal

This is good, and it is pleasing in the sight of God our Saviour, who desires all people to be saved and to come to the knowledge of the truth.

1 Timothy 2: 3-4

elective

———

'I have manifested your name to the people whom you gave me out of the world. Yours they were, and you gave them to me, and they have kept your word.'

universal + elective

Several chapters within this section could easily fall under a more general heading of God's sovereign nature and our human responsibility. The apparent problem might go like this: if God is all-powerful and already has eternity planned, then why does it matter what we do? In other words, how could our daily thoughts and actions have any influence on God's predetermined plans? In this chapter, 'Universal + Elective', we consider the importance of our present response to God's predestined call on our lives. In the following three chapters, 'Master + Messenger', 'Perseverance + Preservation', and 'Decided + Unfolding', we explore the same underlying theme in the context of evangelism, sanctification and prayer (respectively).

We must begin this chapter with an important distinction: there are those who would suggest that, in the end, all people will be saved, irrespective of their beliefs or behaviour. This idea is called 'universalism'. A quick reading of verses such as Colossians 1:20 and Romans 5:19 appear to support the idea.

For in him all the fullness of God was pleased to dwell, and through him to reconcile to himself all things, whether on earth or in heaven, making peace by the blood of his cross. (Col. 1:19-20)

For as by the one man's disobedience the many were made sinners, so by the one man's obedience the many will be made righteous. (Rom. 5:19)

However, on closer inspection, any hope for the salvation of all is difficult to support. In Colossians 1:20, reconciliation is not synonymous with salvation—just as reconciliation brings some to salvation, it also excludes the rebellious from creating further havoc in the new heavens and earth. And, in Romans 5:19, 'all' refers to 'all who receive' (qualified in verse 17), which we know is not everyone. Although one might understandably wish universalism to be true, it's simply not what the Bible teaches.

'Enter by the narrow gate. For the gate is wide and the way is easy that leads to destruction, and those who enter by it are many. For the gate is narrow and the way is hard that leads to life, and those who find it are few.' (Matt. 7:13-14)

Jesus did not believe that all would be saved. Hence the term 'universal' (used here) represents the truth that God *desires* for all to be saved—not that all *will* be saved.

Have I any pleasure in the death of the wicked, declares the LORD God, and not rather that he should turn from his way and live? (Ezek. 18:23)

(God our Saviour) who desires all people to be saved and to come to the knowledge of the truth. (1 Tim. 2:4)

This clarification brings us to an awkward junction—that despite God's universal 'desire' for all to be saved, it is clear this will not happen—not all are selected for salvation:

'I have manifested your name to the people whom you gave me out of the world. Yours they were, and you gave them to me, and they have kept your word.' (John 17:6)

... even as he chose us in him before the foundation of the world, that we should be holy and blameless before him. In love he predestined us for adoption as sons through Jesus Christ, according to the purpose of his will... (Eph. 1:4-5)

The tension between these passages is palpable. Although the heart of God is for all to be saved, He nevertheless knows this will not happen, and has only chosen some—His elect people—to salvation. How can this be? Is God then not powerful enough to fulfil His desire to save everyone? Or is He perhaps not as kind and concerned for us as we had hoped?

This tension appears to present an impossible conflict in the will of an all-powerful God. To understand how we might begin to resolve it, we need to know something fundamental about the operation of God's will.

God has both a 'will of precept' and a 'will of decree'. There are some things that God desires in general, such as goodness. These general desires of God's will exist within His 'will of precept'. An example of God's 'will of precept' would be the general laws and commandments He gives us. We have the capacity to obey these precepts or not. There are other things that God decrees specifically, such as particular events in history. These will happen whether we try to resist them or not. These events can be understood distinctly as part of God's 'will of decree'. He decrees that they happen, and because He is sovereign, they do. So God can be seen to operate with both a 'will of precept' and a 'will of decree'. The pattern we see throughout the Bible is that God's 'will of decree' often appears to contradict His 'will of precept'. In other words, God sometimes permits events to happen which appear to conflict with His general desires.

When God decreed the hardening of Pharaoh's heart, for example, it led directly to sin—which we know is contrary to God's general precepts. Nevertheless, despite this apparently contradictory decree, it was a necessary event to deliver the Israelites out of Egypt and bring about God's more extensive plan of redemption. Perhaps the most significant Biblical evidence of God's will of decree appearing at odds with His will of precept can be seen in the death of Jesus. We are told that all the details (Judas' betrayal, the deceit and hypocrisy of the Jews, the unjust killing by the Romans) were due to God's 'definite plan and foreknowledge' (Acts 2:23). The crucifixion of Jesus, therefore, could not have happened without human sin. In other words, for God to ordain the cross (from which He brought about the salvation of the world), there is a sense in which He also had to ordain the sinful actions leading up to it. Although God never sins or tempts others to sin (James 1:13), somehow, in His infinite wisdom, He uses our wrongful actions to work towards His broader purposes for good. As Paul notes:

And we know that for those who love God all things work together for good, for those who are called according to his purpose. (Rom. 8:28)

The weight of biblical evidence, then, reveals a pattern that God may permit certain things contrary to His will of precept, in order to fulfil some higher commitment. In the case of the cross, God permitted sinful events to fulfil a higher commitment to His wider plan of redemption.

If we apply this precedent to the problem of 'election', it would seem logical that God could desire for all to be saved (as a general precept of His will), while only electing some to salvation (by specific decree) because of that same higher commitment. God's higher commitment is always to His own glory, which is a critical part of His wider plan of redemption. In that sense, the salvation of all humanity is constrained to an elect people by God's higher commitment to the display of His own glory, as revealed in His saving grace to us. And not only is God most glorified through His redemptive plan but also, in the process, Jesus and His redeemed people are glorified:

For it was fitting that he, for whom and by whom all things exist, in bringing many sons to glory, should make the founder of their salvation perfect through suffering. (Heb. 2:10)

The language used in several places in Scripture (in John's gospel in particular) is that God promises a redeemed people to Christ on account of His suffering. Our salvation, in that sense, could be seen primarily as a gift from Father to Son—a gift for Jesus' redemptive work on the cross.

When Jesus had spoken these words, he lifted up his eyes to heaven, and said, 'Father, the hour has come; glorify your Son that the Son may glorify you, since you have given him authority over all flesh, to give eternal life to all whom you have given him.' (John 17:1-2)

Although this still may not help us fully understand how God's elective purposes reveal His glory to the fullest, there is still great merit in attempting to resolve the mystery as far as we can. It benefits our faith greatly to simply hold in tension that God both desires for all to be saved and, at the same time, elects only some for salvation.

Firstly, the truth that God elects anyone at all—that the Creator of the universe chooses us—is in itself incredible. God could have chosen to save no one. He was under no obligation to save us.

But who are you, O man, to answer back to God? Will what is moulded say to its moulder, 'Why have you made me like this?' Has the potter no right over the clay, to make out of the same lump one vessel for honourable use and another for dishonourable use? (Rom. 9:20-21)

That God would redeem any of humanity—and at so high a cost to Him—should fill us with wonder, love and praise.

Secondly, and perhaps easier to reconcile, is the importance of knowing that God desires for all to be saved. If He was unconcerned for the lost, it would call His goodness into question. It is important, therefore, to remember that God is good to all of humanity, whether elect or not. Every creature is given life by God. In that unwarranted existence, however short, we receive through creation enough evidence of God that we might come to repentance.

For his invisible attributes, namely, his eternal power and divine nature, have been clearly perceived, ever since the creation of the world, in the things that have been made. So they are without excuse. (Rom. 1:20)

In this way, God reveals His divinity in nature and leaves us without excuse to receive salvation. He longs for all to repent and receive the full riches of His saving grace:

The Lord is not slow to fulfil his promise as some count slowness, but is patient toward you, not wishing that any should perish, but that all should reach repentance. (2 Pet. 3:9)

So from Scripture, we can be confident of the following: God's general goodness towards all of humanity; His specific longing for all to be saved; and, finally, the inescapable evidence of His divine nature.

These truths effectively bring God's eternal election plans colliding into our present moment. Since we do not share God's omniscience and, therefore, cannot foresee who is part of the elect, we each have a simple choice to make: do we repent and receive His offer of salvation, or not?

master

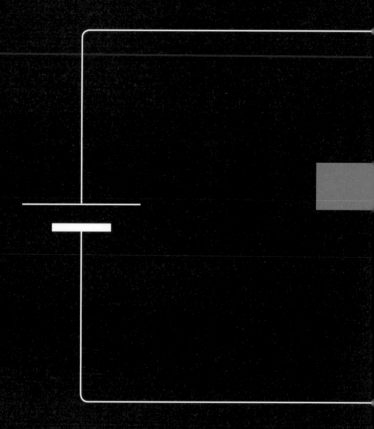

messenger

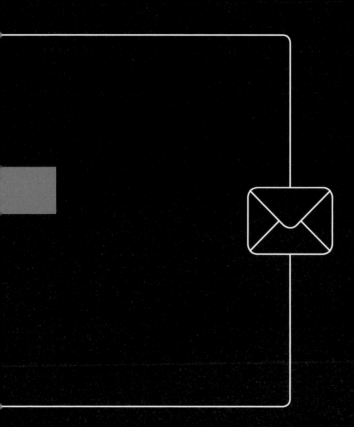

2 Corinthians 5:20

Therefore, we are ambassadors for Christ, God making his appeal through us. We implore you on behalf of Christ, be reconciled to God.

master + messenger

The Bible presents God as the sovereign king and ruler of the universe. He is in control of all events (Isa. 46:10), and it is only by His hand that we are saved (John 6:44). Despite that truth, we are called to be actively involved in that process of salvation, not just to make our own personal response to God (John 6:40), but also to bring His message to others. In the context of evangelism, then, God is the master, and we are His messengers:

'Go therefore and make disciples of all nations, baptising them in the name of the Father and of the Son and of the Holy Spirit, teaching them to observe all that I have commanded you. And behold, I am with you always, to the end of the age.' (Matt. 28:19-20)

The words 'to the end of the age' make it clear that this commandment to be messengers of the gospel is not a one-time instruction for the first disciples. It calls to us to carry on this work today. And yet, if we don't understand the relationship between God's sovereign nature and our human responsibility, we can easily lose our motive to carry on the work as instructed. All of us, whether we do it consciously or not, tend to lean too heavily towards one side of this relationship or the other. Problems arise in both cases:

If we focus too much on God's sovereignty (in other words: God is fully in control; He already knows who'll be saved and it's only by His authority this happens), then we tend to assume it doesn't much matter if we share the gospel or not. God's already decided who's on the list so we can confidently leave all the work to Him.

On the other hand, if we lean too heavily on our human responsibility (in other words: it's mostly our efforts that bring people to faith), then we can easily wind up evangelising for personal motive. We run around, desperately trying to make conversions without dependence on God. If we're doing well, we are tempted towards self-righteousness and pride. In this case, our motive for sharing the gospel often becomes self-centred, and for many, can quickly become a means to appeasing God, even earning salvation by our own efforts. Furthermore, if we happen to doubt our own abilities, we're inclined to leave evangelism to the many ordained and more mature Christians in the church. With that mindset, we effectively absolve all responsibility to be faithful messengers of the gospel. We're happy to leave the work to the more godly.

So how do we maintain a healthy balance in this inevitable tension? How do we reconcile God's limitless power with our necessary human efforts?

Consider for a moment someone hitting a great shot in tennis. Now we could talk about that shot purely from the player's perspective. We might describe their back-swing or their power or timing. In another sense, we could talk about the same shot purely from the perspective of the racquet (the instrument itself). In this case, we might describe the tension in the strings or the strength of the graphite frame.

In the same way, the Bible often talks about only the player (and that's God's sovereign hand—His power to save) and other times only the racquet (and that's us—our physical action to present the gospel). However, both His power and our action are necessary ingredients. In a few places, the Bible talks about both together. In so doing, it reveals how both player and instrument are to work perfectly together in unison. As Jesus explains:

'But you will receive power when the Holy Spirit has come upon you, and you will be my witnesses in Jerusalem and in all Judea and Samaria, and to the end of the earth.' (Acts 1:8)

So the power comes from God and the witnessing—the physical action—is done by us in the power He supplies. Paul explains this relationship to the church, describing how God's Spirit works 'through us':

Therefore, we are ambassadors for Christ, God making his appeal through us. We implore you on behalf of Christ, be reconciled to God. (2 Cor. 5:20)

So this is the biblical model of how we should relate God's sovereign nature with our human responsibility: we have God's power working through us. The sovereign God is alive in the actions of His faithful messenger. This is one of the reasons the Holy Spirit lives in us: so that God can empower our actions through His Spirit. The Father does the drawing, but what a great and humbling privilege to be an instrument in that process. As Samuel Brengle (former Salvation Army commissioner) recognised:

'The axe cannot boast of the trees it has cut down. It could do nothing but for the woodsman. He made it, he sharpened it, and he used it. The moment he throws it aside; it becomes only old iron. O that I may never lose sight of this.'

perseverance

Therefore, since we are surrounded by so great a cloud
of witnesses, let us also lay aside every weight, and sin
which clings so closely, and let us run with endurance the
race that is set before us...

Hebrews 12:1

preservation

Philippians 1:6

And I am sure of this, that he who began a good work in you will bring it to completion at the day of Jesus Christ.

perseverance + preservation

The Bible reminds us often of our need to persevere in faith:

... let us also lay aside every weight, and sin which clings so closely, and let us run with endurance the race that is set before us. (Heb. 12:1)

I press on toward the goal for the prize of the upward call of God in Christ Jesus. (Phil. 3:14)

However, it's also clear from Scripture that God holds us in His hands and preserves our faith to its completion:

And I am sure of this, that he who began a good work in you will bring it to completion at the day of Jesus Christ. (Phil. 1:6)

So this is the tension as it is presented: we must run the race with endurance, even though God has already ensured that we will finish the race. This apparent contradiction between our perseverance and God's preservation raises two immediate questions: firstly, why do we have to persevere at all if God already has our future inheritance secured; and secondly, if we then decide to stop persevering, can we then lose our salvation?

Although these are important questions to ask, we need to see that they don't make sense! The reason for this is surprisingly simple: God enables our perseverance and uses it as the means to preserve us. In other words, God's preservation of us—and our perseverance—is effectively the same thing. They are two sides of the same coin.

Therefore, my beloved, as you have always obeyed, so now, not only as in my presence but much more in my absence, work out your own salvation with fear and trembling, for it is God who works in you, both to will and to work for his good pleasure. (Phil. 2:12-13)

Since God works in us to cause our perseverance, we cannot fail to be preserved by Him. Once we are justified, we can no more stop persevering than the sun can stop shining. Paul helps make this assurance clear for us, revealing that God's preservation is always in place. He will complete the final glorification of anyone who has been predestined:

And those whom he predestined he also called, and those whom he called he also justified, and those whom he justified he also glorified. (Rom. 8:30)

The Westminster Confession of Faith states: 'this perseverance of the saints depends not upon their own free will, but upon the immutability of the decree of election...' In many ways, this doctrine might be more accurately called 'the preservation of the saints', since God does all the heavy lifting. Either way, the doctrine underlines the immutability of our position.

This truth immediately resolves one of our key questions: 'can we lose our salvation if we stop persevering?' The answer, clearly, is 'yes'. We can lose our salvation if we stop persevering, but the true Christian cannot stop persevering because God never stops preserving. For the many professing Christians that do fall by the wayside, the only possible conclusion we can draw is that they were never genuinely born of Christ. The Bible makes this reality very clear in several places:

They went out from us, but they were not of us; for if they had been of us, they would have continued with us. But they went out, that it might become plain that they all are not of us. (1 John 2:19)

Not everyone who says to me, 'Lord, Lord', will enter the kingdom of heaven, but the one who does the will of my Father who is in heaven. (Matt. 7:21)

This is a sobering reality to face. Especially since we've probably all experienced periods when we feel distant from God, or when our belief seems to be hanging on a thread. If we haven't yet experienced these low points, we must at least be prepared for them, and note with humility that even Simon Peter stumbled and disowned Jesus:

'Simon, Simon, behold, Satan demanded to have you, that he might sift you like wheat, but I have prayed for you that your faith may not fail. And when you have turned again, strengthen your brothers.' (Luke 22: 31-32)

Notice how God's sovereign power operates to preserve Peter through a period when his faith and perseverance have faltered. To that end, we should note with great thanksgiving and relief, that God's preservation is a solid bedrock—even when our human perseverance appears fragile and at its weakest point. With Jesus on our side, advocating on our behalf to the Father, we cannot fail to persevere to glory.

Given this certainty, we might well ask the question: why does the Bible still command our perseverance? There are at least three helpful responses we can make to this:

Firstly, the perseverance that Paul often encourages in his letters to the church is not always related to our salvation. In other words, the outcome of such perseverance has no bearing on our salvation, which God has made secure. What then is Paul disciplining his body for, and running towards like an athlete? There are two judgements outlined in the Bible: the white throne judgement (after which, the saved and the unsaved go their separate ways); and, the judgement seat of Christ (where rewards, identified as crowns, are given to the saved on account of their works). When Paul talks about potentially being disqualified if he does not keep up the good fight (1 Cor. 9:27) he is referring to his rewards in heaven, rather than the possibility of losing his salvation. This truth should give us both comfort and motive in our daily struggles.

Secondly, although God enables our ability to persevere, we have also been given moral agency and the responsibility to make good choices. God gives us warnings and commands in the Bible to ensure our preservation. God's people will, therefore, choose to heed these warnings and persevere in the ongoing battle to uproot sin from their lives.

Thirdly, our very ability to persevere is itself a gift from God (Eph. 2:8) that needs to be received. God has given us the gift of faith in order that we might believe. This same gift of faith also has the power to help us go on believing. In that sense, just as God's promise secures our preservation, so God's power enables our perseverance.

(We) who by God's power are being guarded through faith for a salvation ready to be revealed in the last time. (1 Pet. 1:5)

The danger of losing sight of God's sustaining hand in our perseverance is that pride may lead us to boast in our human endeavour. On the other hand, if we simply sit back and make no human effort to persevere at all, then we neglect to make use of the gift God has given us.

Therefore, in conclusion, the key to having peace in this tension is to understand that our ability to endure is a gift from God—a gift that the Bible commands us to put into action. So as we persevere, we can be thankful to God that, by His grace, He enables our very ability to do so. In that sense, God can be seen to preserve us—and we to persevere—both on account of His great power and mercy.

Now to him who is able to keep you from stumbling and to present you blameless before the presence of his glory with great joy, to the only God, our Saviour, through Jesus Christ our Lord, be glory, majesty, dominion, and authority, before all time and now and for ever. Amen. (Jude 1:24-25)

decided

Declaring the end from the beginning and from ancient times things not yet done, saying, 'My counsel shall stand, and I will accomplish all my purpose.'

Isaiah 46:10

unfolding

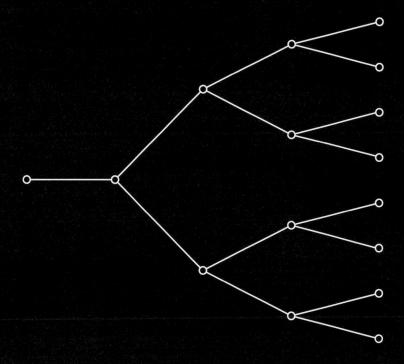

2 Corinthians 1:11 (MSG)

I can see your faces even now, lifted in praise for God's deliverance of us, a rescue in which your prayers played such a crucial part.

decided + unfolding

_____

He has made everything beautiful in its time. Also, he has put eternity into man's heart, yet so that he cannot find out what God has done from the beginning to the end. (Eccles. 3:11)

We have a God who is omniscient, who has both foreknowledge and control of all events in history (Isa. 46:10). The future is decided. So, we might well ask, can we change the future through our present actions? Or more specifically, can our prayers of petition change God's mind? If everything is already decided, what point is there in prayer?

In a fascinating exchange in Genesis 18, Abraham prays to God and intercedes on behalf of the people in Sodom. God had set out His intention to wipe out the city. Abraham then calls on God to change His mind, humbly questioning whether it would be fair to wipe out the entire city if some righteous people were still living there. He begins with an arbitrary figure of fifty righteous:

'Suppose there are fifty righteous within the city. Will you then sweep away the place and not spare it for the fifty righteous who are in it?' (Gen. 18:24)

God agrees that if there were fifty righteous people, He would spare the whole city on their behalf (wicked and righteous). This mercy is clearly more than Abraham had bargained for—he would perhaps only have been hoping for the righteous to be spared. God, however, will spare them all on account of the fifty righteous. Encouraged by this show of mercy, Abraham then begins to barter, in increments of ten, until God agrees that He would spare the whole place for even ten righteous. Abraham stops there, but we can imagine that God would have gone further—even to spare all the wicked for just one righteous person. God's ultimate plan of redemption is foreshadowed here: that God would spare us all through faith in the one and only righteous man to live, Jesus Christ. In the case of Sodom, what Abraham overlooks, and what God knows, is that nobody living there is righteous, not one (Rom. 3:10). Sodom is destroyed.

Abraham's prayer doesn't change God's mind. No prayer in the Bible ever changes God's mind. Jesus understood this better than anyone. This truth is made plain in the Garden of Gethsemane. When facing death, Jesus pleads to God to take the cup of wrath from Him, but adds the all-important words, 'yet not my will be done but yours'.

At this point, we need to make an important philosophical distinction. There is a notable difference between our prayers changing history—and—our prayers changing God's mind. God is unchangeable and knows all things; however, this does not necessarily limit our ability to change the future through our present actions. This could be best understood as a future that God has already planned, which makes allowance for our present actions. In other words, the future is already decided by God but is unfolding through our actions. This certainty should be a great comfort to us. We know the final destination, the end goal; and through our participation in the present, God brings our plan to pass.

In that sense, although our prayers do not change God's mind, they do change history. Paul, writing to the church in Corinth about his escape from prison, explains perfectly how our prayers do make a difference:

We don't want you in the dark, friends, about how hard it was when all this came down on us in Asia province. It was so bad we didn't think we were going to make it. We felt like we'd been sent to death row, that it was all over for us. As it turned out, it was the best thing that could have happened. Instead of trusting in our own strength or wits to get out of it, we were forced to trust God totally—not a bad idea since he's the God who raises the dead! And he did it, rescued us from certain doom. And he'll do it again, rescuing us as many times as we need rescuing. You and your prayers are part of the rescue operation—I don't want you in the dark about that either. I can see your faces even now, lifted in praise for God's deliverance of us, a rescue in which your prayers played such a crucial part. (2 Cor. 1:8-11 MSG)

We see similar evidence of the impact of prayer when Herod imprisons Peter:

So Peter was kept in prison, but earnest prayer for him was made to God by the church. (Acts 12:5)

His subsequent escape is a miracle of God, brought about in response to the prayers of His people. This kind of intercessory prayer is selfless—other-centred—and although we might imagine that God ranks such prayer higher than our own personal pleas, we can establish from Scripture that God may also choose to answer the most seemingly self-centred prayers. In the book of 2 Kings, for example, we see God answer King Hezekiah's fearful prayers to avoid imminent death, resulting in a fifteen-year extension to his life:

'Turn back, and say to Hezekiah the leader of my people, Thus says the LORD, the God of David your father: I have heard your prayer; I have seen your tears. Behold, I will heal you. On the third day you shall go up to the house of the Lord, and I will add fifteen years to your life.' (2 Kings 20:5-6)

We should note, however, from the following verse, that the prayer was primarily answered for God's glory, and for David's (from whose line salvation would come through Jesus):

'... and I will add fifteen years to your life. I will deliver you and this city out of the hand of the king of Assyria, and I will defend this city for my own sake and for my servant David's sake.'
(2 Kings 20:6)

God gets the glory; but as His children, He desires for us to recognise His sovereign hand in our lives and seek His help in all things:

The Lord is at hand; do not be anxious about anything, but in everything by prayer and supplication with thanksgiving let your requests be made known to God. (Phil. 4:6)

In summary, the overriding evidence of Scripture is that our prayers make a difference—no matter how seemingly self-centred or trivial in context—they bring us personally closer to God through relationship. Furthermore, if we're praying with the right heart (James 4:2-3), we have the potential to change history and move towards a future, known to God. Though not always answered as we might expect, God ordains our prayers to bring His plans to pass.

Our joy and hope in prayer, therefore, should be set on the reality that through our reliance on God, not only do we give glory and recognition to Him, but we can also give great blessing and comfort to each other in the process.

It is no wonder then that we are instructed to pray. To have a continual dialogue—a living relationship with our Lord. In so doing, we are obediently carrying out God's plan for us.

Rejoice in hope, be patient in tribulation, be constant in prayer. (Rom. 12:12)

Knowing that both sides of this apparent contradiction are equally true and necessary is essential for our spiritual journey. That God has already decided the future should give us great stability, assurance and comfort. That this same future is unfolding through our prayers and actions should highlight the importance of our ongoing engagement with the living God.

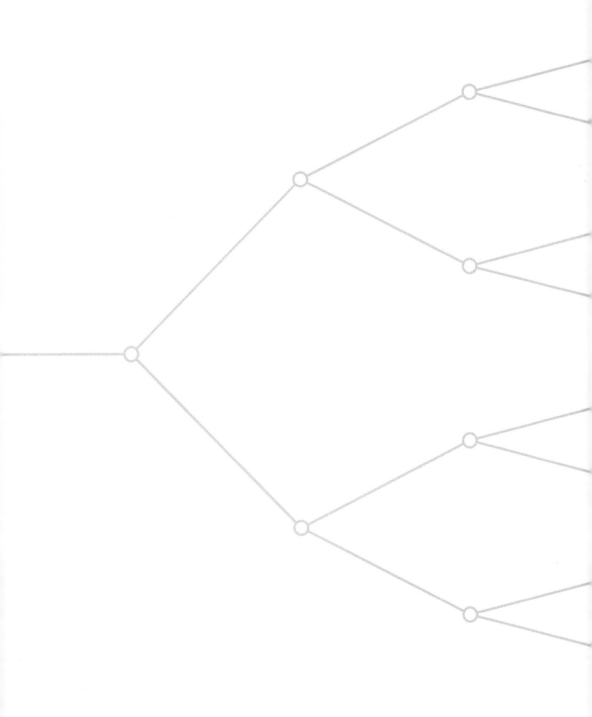

death

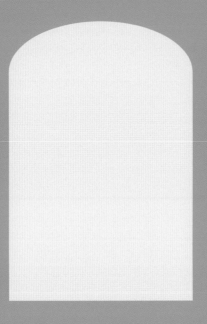

Do you not know that all of us who have been baptised into Christ Jesus were baptised into his death?

Romans 6:3

life

John 3:3

Jesus answered him, 'Truly, truly, I say to you, unless one is born again he cannot see the kingdom of God.'

death + life

_____

In John chapter 3, one of the Jewish leaders, a man called Nicodemus, professes that Jesus must be the Son of God because of the signs He is producing. In response to this, Jesus tells the man that he must be born again to see the kingdom of God. We can imagine the confusion this must have caused. In a slightly comical statement, Nicodemus questions how a grown man could re-enter his mother's womb to be born a second time! With hindsight, we can understand what Jesus meant: that one must be born again 'of the Spirit'. Jesus explains this reality to Nicodemus:

'Truly, truly, I say to you, unless one is born of water and the Spirit, he cannot enter the kingdom of God. That which is born of the flesh is flesh, and that which is born of the Spirit is spirit. Do not marvel that I said to you, "You must be born again."' (John 3:5-7)

So what exactly does it mean to be born again 'of the Spirit'? To understand this, we must first understand how we were created. After the initial creation story in Genesis chapter 1, the focus shifts to humanity, emphasising our spiritual capacity:

Then the LORD God formed the man of dust from the ground and breathed into his nostrils the breath of life, and the man became a living creature. (Gen. 2:7)

The concept of the created human being is that we were formed from the soil and brought into being by God's breath. The *Pulpit Commentary* puts it like this:

'Man received his life from a distinct act of Divine inbreathing; certainly not an in-breathing of atmospheric air, but an inflatus from the Ruach Elohim, or Spirit of God, a communication from the whole personality of the Godhead.'

Through this specific impartation of God's life-giving Spirit, a spiritual dimension was created in humanity. This 'inflatus' makes us distinct from the rest of creation. Like all the animals, we have a body, with mind, will and emotions. Setting us apart, however, is that we also have a spirit—a vertical dimension connecting our embodied souls to God.

One of the many influences of Greek thinking on our culture is the distinct separation of the material and immaterial. In the New Testament, the 'immaterial' parts of a being (spirit and soul) are often grouped and referenced interchangeably. The legacy of this thinking promotes a natural divide in our current thinking between the physical body and the spirit or soul. We should note that the Hebrew understanding of the human soul was a more unified entity with less emphasis on the divisions between the elements. This understanding is helpful, as it reminds us that the separation of body and soul, which occurs at our physical death, is merely an 'unnatural tragedy which will be remedied when the body is resurrected, allowing humans to exist as they were intended to do.' *(ESV Study Bible)*

God's redemption plan includes the restoration of the whole creation, which includes our whole being—body and spirit—though we must recognise that body and spirit are not reborn at the same time. The spirit is reborn first.

At this point, we might well ask: if God has already made us with a spirit, why then must we be reborn of the Spirit? The answer is explained by the fall of Adam:

Therefore, just as sin came into the world through one man, and death through sin, and so death spread to all men because all sinned. (Rom. 5:12)

The Apostle Paul explains that when we are born physically from the womb, our spiritual life is already dead. In that sense, humanity is like the walking dead until spiritual rebirth occurs.

And you were dead in the trespasses and sins in which you once walked, following the course of this world, following the prince of the power of the air, the spirit that is now at work in the sons of disobedience. (Eph. 2:1-2)

Calvin summarises helpfully in his commentary: '[Paul] does not mean simply that they were in danger of death; but he declares that it was a real and present death under which they laboured. As spiritual death is nothing else than the alienation of the soul from God, we are all born as dead men, and we live as dead men, until we are made partakers of the life of Christ.'

The good news, as Calvin begins to explain, is that Christ's obedience reverses Adam's disobedience. It brings new life, where there was once only death.

For as by a man came death, by a man has come also the resurrection of the dead. For as in Adam all die, so also in Christ shall all be made alive. (1 Cor. 15:21-22)

Therefore as partakers of the life of Christ, we are once again made alive in the Spirit. At this point, we might say, 'hallelujah—the end!' ... but there's more—we also have the rebirth of our physical bodies to look forward to:

For we know that when this earthly tent we live in is taken down (that is, when we die and leave this earthly body), we will have a house in heaven, an eternal body made for us by God himself and not by human hands. We grow weary in our present bodies, and we long to put on our heavenly bodies like new clothing. For we will put on heavenly bodies; we will not be spirits without bodies. While we live in these earthly bodies, we groan and sigh, but it's not that we want to die and get rid of these bodies that clothe us. Rather, we want to put on our new bodies so that these dying bodies will be swallowed up by life. (2 Corinthians 5:1-4 NLT)

In this passage, the earthly tent Paul refers to represents the body. The exciting revelation is that God has a new body in store for us. This new body is in line with God's restoration plan to bring down a new heaven and a new earth (Rev. 21:1). We will not be floating around like ghosts in the clouds. We will have a new body, on a new earth. How much our new resurrection bodies may resemble our current body cannot be definitively known from Scripture; however, as with our spirit, there is a clear sense that this new birth is a process of renewal and regeneration. Just as the charred remains of a dead forest are swallowed up by the soil, only to burst into new life; so too our bodies will undergo a cycle of death and rebirth: something old, clothed in something new, which transforms us, you and I… the same you and I… but different. Imperishable.

So through God's restoration plan for humanity, the Bible gives us this incredible bird's eye view of the cycle of life and death in our beings. Remembering that there is both death and life contained in the unfolding miracle of being reconciled to God is hugely important in our daily walk of faith.

If we only dwell in a cycle of death—of personal self-denial—then the path becomes arid and eventually hopeless. The Spirit brings hope, and through hope, joy and abundant life (John 10:10). Furthermore, since our death is 'in Christ', we are subsequently brought to new life as a people 'for Christ'. In this rebirth, we are granted union with God—Christ living in us.

I have been crucified with Christ. It is no longer I who live, but Christ who lives in me. And the life I now live in the flesh I live by faith in the Son of God, who loved me and gave himself for me. (Gal. 2:20)

On the other hand, to seek only life—without the death of the old self—is to live in disillusionment. C.S. Lewis says: 'A rejection, or in Scripture's strong language, a crucifixion of the natural self is the passport to everlasting life. Nothing that has not died will be resurrected.' Without recognising this need for the death of the old self, we trivialise what it cost Jesus on the cross. Our new life is only made possible through partaking in His death. The grace He offers us did not come cheaply.

We were buried therefore with him by baptism into death, in order that, just as Christ was raised from the dead by the glory of the Father, we too might walk in newness of life. (Rom. 6:4)

We must, therefore, heed the gravity of our calling to take on Christ's death, as well as His resurrection life, or the Christian life has no substance.

New life cannot be accessed without death.

blessings

'And all these blessings shall come upon you and overtake you, if you obey the voice of the LORD your God.'

Deuteronomy 28:2

curses

Galatians 3:13

Christ redeemed us from the curse of the law by becoming a curse for us—for it is written, 'Cursed is everyone who is hanged on a tree.'

blessings + curses

Scripture is full of references to blessings and curses. From the very first book in the Bible, we repeatedly witness humanity being blessed or cursed depending on their faithfulness to God. The pattern we see emerging is that God's response to His people always relates to His covenant promises with them. Understanding, therefore, how blessings and curses operate in the context of covenant theology is crucial. It remains as important today as it was 4000 years ago, and gives us one of the richest veins through which to mine the gospel, illuminating it in all its brilliance.

God makes several promises with His people throughout history. Most of these are part of the same overarching promise, called God's covenant of grace. The covenant of grace is the central theme and narrative to the entire Bible. It is God's promise of a rescue plan for humanity and our groaning world. It is inaugurated in Genesis 3:15 with the promise that the 'seed' of the woman (Jesus) would crush the serpent's head.

God renews His covenant of grace on several occasions with key representatives in history, including Abraham, Moses, David and finally Jesus. We could understand this as a series of updates to the same core agreement. Although the final update with Jesus is often referred to as the 'new covenant', it should be understood in context as the closing agreement in God's one overarching covenant of grace.

It's important to note that the basic structure of each agreement remains the same. Each contains a set of conditions to uphold. If the conditions are kept, blessings are received; if the conditions are broken, curses are received. So, it's fairly straightforward: if we do what we agree to do, we get blessed; if we break our promise, we get cursed. In that sense, blessings and curses are always necessary components of God's promises. It's helpful to observe that the conditions, the blessings and the curses remain essentially the same throughout the entire covenant of grace. The condition is always faith; the blessing is always to be with God in paradise; and finally, the curse is always separation from God's favour.

If we looked at each covenant update more closely, we would notice how the detail of the agreement expands and develops with each update. So for example, the paradise where God promises to dwell with His people moves from Canaan, to Jerusalem, to our hearts (the Holy Spirit dwelling within us), and finally, to a new heaven and a new earth in the age to come. The curse of separation from God's favour would initially have meant exile from the promised land but, in the final covenant update with Jesus, the curse is hell—a complete separation from His grace.

Setting aside the development of the details over time, the critical thing to see is that the entire Bible rings out with this same overarching narrative: God promises to dwell with a faithful people in paradise. Look at the consistency of the promise over the following cross-section of Scripture:

'And I will give to you and to your offspring after you the land of your sojournings, all the land of Canaan, for an everlasting possession, and I will be their God.' (Gen. 17:8)

'My dwelling place shall be with them, and I will be their God, and they shall be my people.' (Ezek. 37:27)

'I will put my law within them, and I will write it on their hearts. And I will be their God, and they shall be my people.' (Jer. 31:33)

'I will make my dwelling among them, and I will walk among them and be their God, and they shall be my people.' (2 Cor. 6:16)

And I heard a loud voice from the throne saying, 'Behold, the dwelling place of God is with man. He will dwell with them, and they will be his people, and God himself will be with them as their God.' (Rev. 21:3)

So how does this covenant of grace continue to make sense to us today? When the Israelites were attempting to live out their covenant promise with God, we witness them, again and again, failing to remain faithful. As a result, they are cursed and suffer exile from the land. Between moments of repentance and subsequent faithfulness, they also receive great blessings from God. They appear to stumble through history in a washing machine of blessings and curses, raising the obvious question: what prevents this cycle of blessings and curses from occurring indefinitely throughout their history, and ours?

The answer is found in Christ.

And he took bread, and when he had given thanks, he broke it and gave it to them, saying, 'This is my body, which is given for you. Do this in remembrance of me.' And likewise the cup after they had eaten, saying, 'This cup that is poured out for you is the new covenant in my blood.' (Luke 22:19-20)

The problem of our ongoing infidelity to God would, in the end, be resolved by God Himself! The new covenant, the final chapter in the one overarching covenant of grace, is made with Christ, with God Himself. It ends our cycle of infidelity, and humanity is effectively taken out of the washing machine and hung up to dry.

To understand how this works in practice, we need to know something specific about the covenant of grace. Despite the various updates in history, the agreement is only officially sealed once. This takes place in the first instalment of the agreement, in a ceremony enacted in Genesis 15 between Abraham (then Abram) and God. After God and Abram enter into this first instalment of the covenant agreement, Abram lines up a corridor of severed animal pieces.

Today, if we make an agreement, we might shake hands on it, or sign a piece of paper, for example. This action represents us binding the agreement personally—putting ourselves 'on the line' so to speak. At that particular period in Israel's history, when two people entered a covenant agreement together, the person of lower rank had to walk between a corridor of dead animal carcasses. This is how they put themselves 'on the line'. Walking between the animal pieces symbolised the curse of the covenant. The person walking through was officially accepting the penalty clause if they broke the agreement. In other words, if the person of lower rank broke his side of the promise, his body would be subject to death—subject to the same fate as the dead animals around them. The shocking surprise in this ceremony is that despite being of lower rank, Abram never actually goes through the corridor of animal pieces. Instead, God goes through. Twice.

... a smoking firepot and a flaming torch passed between these pieces. On that day the LORD made a covenant with Abram.... (Gen. 15:17-18)

The significance of God going through the animal pieces twice should not be lost on us. It means that not only will God take the curse of the covenant if He breaks His side of the bargain; He'll also take the curse if we break our side of the bargain. In other words, what God is saying to us today, through this one covenant of grace, is this: I will be your God, and you will be My people; and, if you cannot uphold your side of the bargain—if you cannot be a faithful people—My body will be broken for you, and My blood will be shed, just like these animals.

Of course, with the benefit of hindsight, we know that His body was broken for us. Two thousand years later, God, in the person of Jesus Christ, died on our behalf to honour this agreement and free us from the curse of the covenant. He not only fulfilled the conditions of the covenant by living a perfectly faithful life (obedient to God to the end); but, He also took the curse of the covenant, dying for our inability to live perfectly faithful lives. He died so that we might be legally free to receive the blessings of the covenant: to be a people with God in paradise.

Christ redeemed us from the curse of the law by becoming a curse for us—for it is written, 'Cursed is everyone who is hanged on a tree.' (Gal. 3:13)

This is incredibly good news for us! It means that when we enter by faith into the final instalment of this same covenant of grace, officially sealed all the way back in Genesis 15, we receive the blessing of being 'a people with God in paradise'. Moreover, the very way in which God is 'with us' today—living by His Spirit in our hearts—is the very thing that breaks our cycle of infidelity, as declared in Jeremiah 31:31–34 and foretold by Moses:

And the LORD your God will circumcise your heart and the heart of your offspring, so that you will love the LORD your God with all your heart and with all your soul, that you may live. (Deut. 30:6)

This is the unexpected blessing that Jesus leaves with us: the Holy Spirit—the presence of God—who by His sanctifying work in our lives, circumcises our hearts and ends our cycle of infidelity. The Spirit also brings unity in the church, which gives us the earthly realm of God's blessing. In that sense, ex-communication from the church (as Paul commands in 1 Cor. 5:13: 'Purge the evil person from among you') is the equivalent of being cursed—exile from God.

We should note, however, that cursing remains a confusing issue for many today. In the Bible, there is evidence of men cursing men, and we see the influence of other spiritual forces negatively affecting people's lives. There is also the reality of the consequences of sin lingering through generations. We know this from David's story (2 Sam. 12:10-14), which reveals how David's life—and his children's lives—are devastatingly impacted after his episode of sin with Bathsheba. We also know this truth by experience—abusive adults are often first abused themselves as children. Sin often has severe repercussions in our lives, and there is constant spiritual warfare going on all around us (2 Cor. 10:4).

None of this, however, should be understood in the context of the ultimate curse of separation from God. Furthermore, when we are in Christ, the Holy Spirit—who is at work in our lives—is more powerful than any other spiritual influence we may encounter. Despite all the brokenness we may face, the critical curse has been lifted, and nothing can separate us from the love of God:

For I am sure that neither death nor life, nor angels nor rulers, nor things present nor things to come, nor powers, nor height nor depth, nor anything else in all creation, will be able to separate us from the love of God in Christ Jesus our Lord. (Rom. 8:38-39)

In conclusion, a covenant-shaped view of blessings and curses should help us see a new abundance of blessing in our lives today. Since blessing is always defined in the covenant as the presence of God, we should recognise blessing every time God is present. By definition then, we are blessed every time we walk in the Spirit; we are blessed every time we pray; we are blessed every time God reveals Himself to us in Scripture; we are blessed every time God reveals Himself to us in nature. Through the body of the church, God especially blesses us that we might be a blessing to others. So then, we are blessed every time our brothers and sisters in Christ encourage us, teach us, admonish us, pray for us, heal us, prophesy over us… in short, blessings are everywhere.

For those who receive Jesus by faith, the curse is removed. Blessings abound!

Thanks be to God.

now

!

Being asked by the Pharisees when the kingdom of God would come, he answered them, 'The kingdom of God is not coming in ways that can be observed, nor will they say, "Look, here it is!" or "There!" for behold, the kingdom of God is in the midst of you.'

Luke 17:20-21

not yet

• • •

1 John 3:2

Beloved, we are God's children now, and what we will be has not yet appeared; but we know that when he appears we shall be like him, because we shall see him as he is.

now + not yet

_____

We live in a strange in-between period in history. Jesus has come, and the decisive victory has been won. Through His work on the cross, we are offered the grace to be free from sin and condemnation, joining the ranks of the kingdom of God. When we repent and are baptised, we are immediately counted as righteous by God. The rest of our lives is then an ongoing process of being conformed in Christ-likeness by the Spirit of God. This process goes on until the day we die—unless Christ returns while we live. Either way, on the day He returns, both the living and the dead in Christ will be raised to new life. On this day, we will be glorified by Christ, who returns as the perfecter of our faith. The time in which we now live falls between these two visits of Christ. We take part in His victory, and yet we live in an imperfect world, looking forward with hope to a time when all things will be made new in His kingdom.

Jesus often spoke about the kingdom of God. The people were desperate to understand the nature and timing of the kingdom, but there remained great confusion. It seems Jesus expected this:

Being asked by the Pharisees when the kingdom of God would come, he answered them, 'The kingdom of God is not coming in ways that can be observed, nor will they say, "Look, here it is!" or "There!" for behold, the kingdom of God is in the midst of you.' (Luke 17:20-21)

Jesus understood that many of the Jews believed the Messiah would come with military might, to introduce His kingdom by force. The simple reality that Jesus was present, however, was evidence that the kingdom was already in their midst. No physical battles to entertain, just a carpenter's son to believe in. Even when they crucified Him it didn't stop the kingdom coming—the seeds had been sown. Something was about to change at the heart level.

For this is the covenant that I will make with the house of Israel after those days, declares the LORD: _I will put my law within them, and I will write it on their hearts. And I will be their God, and they shall be my people. (Jer. 31:33)_

In the sense in which Jesus interpreted Scripture, our access to the kingdom could be defined as having the presence of God living in us. Perhaps not surprisingly then, Jesus taught us to pray for His kingdom to come (Luke 11:2). No sharpening of swords, just a command to pray. He explained, through the parable of the mustard seed, how the kingdom was already planted and ready for growth. It would grow like a quiet, slow revolution—starting small but eventually becoming vast:

'The kingdom of heaven is like a grain of mustard seed that a man took and sowed in his field. It is the smallest of all seeds, but when it has grown it is larger than all the garden plants and becomes a tree, so that the birds of the air come and make nests in its branches.' (Matt. 13:31-32)

This parable gives us a picture of the timing of God's kingdom: it is already planted and in our midst but will not reach its full expression until some future point. Theologians speak about the kingdom as being been inaugurated, but not yet consummated. George Eldon Ladd (in *The Gospel of the Kingdom*) argues that the kingdom should be understood as a rule, rather than purely a realm. The 'kingdom of God', therefore, could be described interchangeably as the 'reign of God'. So rather than a purely physical territory, it is anywhere where God rules.

This notion of 'reign' is a helpful distinction when we consider how the kingdom is both now and not yet. Where Jesus walked, He carried out the will of the Father with perfect obedience. God reigned in His earthly life. In that sense, the kingdom was in the midst of the people in Jesus' time. When Jesus ascended to the Father, He sent us a helper, the Spirit of God (John 14:26). Through faith in Jesus, the Spirit brings us into the kingdom.

He has delivered us from the domain of darkness and transferred us to the kingdom of his beloved Son. (Col. 1:13)

Despite living in an age of relative darkness, the people of God can, therefore, bring the kingdom of God into this chaos. In that sense, the church provides an earthly glimpse of the kingdom of God—where the presence of God abounds and the King reigns.

The difficulty we face, of course, is that we struggle to remain in God's presence. The kingdom is often not very evident within us, let alone in the broken world around us. So we rightly desire to see more of the kingdom now and, as Jesus taught us to pray, we ask for His kingdom to come. This is a good and natural response—to seek more of the kingdom now—but it brings with it a particular danger: many kingdom blessings can be experienced today, but many are reserved for the consummation and final coming of Jesus. A deficit between expectation and experience can sometimes leave people blaming God, or themselves.

Our understandable desire to experience more of the kingdom now must be held in tension with the reality that it has not yet come in full. Jesus warned of the frightening outcome for many who would be swept into the power of God's kingdom now—today—but never see its final consummation. The 'parable of the net' in Matthew 13 gives us the picture of many people being swept into the kingdom—performing kingdom work—but never knowing God, and eventually being exposed as frauds.

On that day many will say to me, 'Lord, Lord, did we not prophesy in your name, and cast out demons in your name, and do many mighty works in your name?' And then will I declare to them, 'I never knew you; depart from me, you workers of lawlessness.' (Matt. 7:22-23)

We can assume, therefore, that not all who are swept into the power of God's kingdom—not all professing Christians in the church—are genuine children of the kingdom. The power of the kingdom gathers many into its net who will be cast out in the end because they loved healing but neglected holiness; they loved power but neglected purity; they loved the wonders of God but neglected the will of God.

So we must be careful, and prayerfully discern whether we are too caught up in the 'now' of the kingdom; or whether by patience, endurance and faithfulness, we also await with hope the 'not yet' of the kingdom, the final consummation of God's reign.

We must observe, however, that there are pitfalls at either extreme. If our sole aim is to hang on doggedly for the 'not yet' (and we completely shut down the 'now' of the kingdom), we will inevitably miss out on the full potential of the Holy Spirit's work in our lives today. In particular, the gifts of the Spirit, with which we might enhance and equip the spiritual lives of others (Eph. 4:12-13). How then can we be a blessing to the church?

Furthermore, without a healthy desire to partake in God's kingdom today, we sacrifice the joy of witnessing God at work first-hand. In this, we miss receiving—as intimated below—some pale idea of the glory we can eagerly anticipate on that exciting day when the kingdom comes in all its fullness.

For now we see in a mirror dimly, but then face to face. Now I know in part; then I shall know fully, even as I have been fully known. (1 Cor. 13:12)

natural

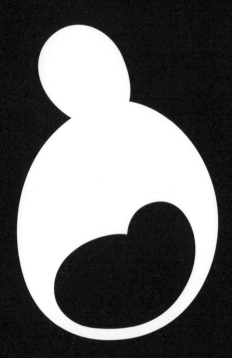

Therefore the Lord himself will give you a sign. Behold, the virgin shall conceive and bear a son, and shall call his name Immanuel.

Isaiah 7:14

supernatural

And Mary said to the angel,
'How will this be, since I am a virgin?'

natural + supernatural

There have been many efforts across history to define the term 'supernatural'. In the sense in which I'm using it here, it could be interchangeable with the term 'miraculous'. A helpful definition at the outset would be that of St Thomas Aquinas, who said: 'those happenings are properly called miraculous which are done by divine agency outside the commonly observed order of things.'

For many, the supernatural is a direct stumbling block to faith. It is the stuff of fairy-tales and fantasy. We have become so advanced that much of what we would previously have described as supernatural, we can now explain scientifically. An oversimplified world view has developed from this confidence, which asserts that all events can be explained scientifically; and what we cannot yet explain, we will soon uncover.

The development of this view took root in the enlightenment period and peaked in the age of modernism. It is fraying around the edges again today for two reasons: firstly, post-modernism engendered a more nuanced, less black-and-white view of the world; secondly, we're currently in the wave of a tech revolution, which is moving so quickly that we barely understand many of the systems operating around us. With both those shifts, we find our daily lives increasingly saturated with the uncertain and the unknown.

The irony of this should not be lost on us: that despite all our advancements, we are now living in a world that is significantly less well known to us.

We can, therefore, already trace a shift in the rather binary view that science will inevitably replace mystery, to a more pluralistic view in which the known and the unknown co-exist more comfortably. In that sense, we might expect people, Christians included, to be more receptive to the supernatural. We might also assume that this contradiction divides itself neatly across the line of faith. In other words, those who embrace religion also embrace the supernatural by default; and, similarly, those who remain sceptical of religion accept only nature.

However, we know by experience this isn't true. There are many highly spiritual people operating outside of the context of organised religion; and, of course, there are many professing Christians who will caveat that they don't believe in certain 'miraculous' aspects of biblical revelation. How many church-goers would struggle to risk their credibility by publicly defending—arguably the most mind-boggling supernatural event of all—the immaculate conception?

And Mary said to the angel, 'How will this be, since I am a virgin?' (Luke 1:34)

That Mary could bear a child and be a virgin at the same time is one of the great mysteries of the Bible. For the sake of the gospel, it can only be understood as a genuine miracle—one of those points in time when the supernatural noticeably invades the natural order of things. For many, it is the first and last stumbling block to faith; shipwrecks of a nativity-marked childhood, only to be grown out of like Santa Claus and the tooth fairy.

It may seem irrational to believe in such a miraculous event; and yet, for God to create time, space and matter out of nothing is arguably a bigger miracle that many find easier to swallow. That Jesus could heal someone in the street or turn water into wine seems infinitely more plausible. However, one thing is certain: if we are prepared to believe that anything miraculous is possible, then we should be prepared to believe that everything miraculous is possible.

The aim, in this short chapter, is not to give evidence (biblical or anecdotal) that the supernatural exists, but rather, to trust the Bible that it does, and to present its relationship with the natural in a more complementary way. In that regard, the framework of 'both-and' is particularly relevant to this apparent contradiction. It is relevant, not just in the sense that both the natural and the supernatural exist, but also because, on a deeper level, all the events we experience can be seen to contain both states. Instead of separating the two, therefore, it is more helpful to understand that both the natural and the supernatural are omnipresent. In other words, rather than any particular experience being entirely natural or supernatural, they are always both.

For many of us, in order to see that both states exist, we need to see them 'in each other'. Some of us need to become better at recognising the supernatural in the natural; and others, to recognise the natural aspect to every supernatural event. Let's consider each in turn.

Firstly, how do we better recognise the supernatural in the natural? Should we find this duality hard to observe, it may well be because we have lost the ability to see as a child, with wonder—to see the miraculous in the mundane. And yet we have such a rich history of doing precisely that. The poetry of the early Irish monks revelled with childlike awe in the enchantment of nature. Their day-to-day reality was saturated with the supernatural, seen through the filter of God's sustaining power at work in creation.

The traces of this vision can be seen in recent Irish poetry, by poets such as Patrick Kavanagh:

Yet sometimes when the sun comes through a gap
These men know God the Father in a tree:
The Holy Spirit is the rising sap,
And Christ will be the green leaves that will come
At Easter from the sealed and guarded tomb.
(From 'The Great Hunger' by Patrick Kavanagh)

One could imagine the original inspiration for this way of viewing the world to be found directly in the Psalms:

The heavens declare the glory of God, and the sky above proclaims his handiwork.
Day to day pours out speech, and night to night reveals knowledge.
There is no speech, nor are there words, whose voice is not heard.
Their voice goes out through all the earth, and their words to the end of the world.
(Ps. 19:1-4)

Since God created the natural world, there is an observable reality that all of the created matter 'speaks' in return to its Creator. This language, which could be identified as the song of creation (Job 38:7), is evident all around us. It is an ongoing dialogue that connects the natural to the supernatural, the earth to its author, and is made plain for humanity to enjoy:

For his invisible attributes, namely, his eternal power and divine nature, have been clearly perceived,
ever since the creation of the world, in the things that have been made... (Rom. 1:20)

When we experience a stunning mountain-top view, or stand in awe at the crashing waves, we are effectively tuning-in to the echo of the divine—the supernatural audible in the natural.

To see the World in a Grain of Sand
And Heaven in a Wild Flower,
Hold Infinity in the palm of your hand
And Eternity in an hour.
(From 'Auguries of Innocence' by William Blake)

Beautiful as these words are, there is a theology that can go askew in such longings. Sometimes we desire to see God so much in the tree, in the wild flower, that we worship the object itself as God—a form of idolatry; or a form of Pantheism—of God in all things rather than God's creative hand in all things. We must be clear that the awe we experience in nature arises only because nature itself points us to the goodness of its Creator.

On a less cosmic and dramatic level, the supernatural can also be evidenced in even the most ordinary event. In the film *Chariots of Fire*, Eric Liddell's father, a missionary and pastor, makes the following statement: 'Eric, you can praise the Lord by peeling a spud, if you peel it to perfection.' In context, he is warning Eric that to glorify God, he must do his work (in this case, his running) to the best of his God-given ability, without compromise. The comparative illustration of 'peeling a spud' is a great one, as it reveals how even our most mundane act can rise in significance as an act of praise and worship to God. It demonstrates perfectly how the day-to-day can be invested with the spiritual—how every natural act has the capacity for the supernatural to be comfortably present as we honour and glorify our Creator.

This means that even a simple, earthly prayer can be invested with unexpected supernatural emphasis. We may have prayed, for example, for healing over someone who's been ill. Instinctively, we consider Jesus' ministry and rightly pray, in His name, for similar acts of miraculous intervention on the patient. Often God in His mercy, according to His will, does intervene, and His name is glorified through this grace. For some, it will be surprisingly less obvious to pray for the skill of the surgeon and the quality of the medical care, not wishing to bank our hopes on apparently more 'natural' remedies.

However, if we consider all creation as both natural and supernatural, it should be no less miraculous (and no less to God's glory), that a surgeon might use his God-given wisdom, insight and skill to perform incredible healing. Even should that surgeon not be a man of faith, God in His common grace and goodness to all of humanity endows us with incredible ability and talents. We are miraculously created by God. More specifically, as His people, we are His possession (Rom. 14:8), and our minds, hands and feet live to the Lord. In that sense, all that we do is laced with the supernatural.

While we may struggle to see the natural as supernatural, it may arguably be even more challenging to do the reverse—to see the supernatural as natural. On coming to faith in God, His Spirit lives in us. Although we might think of much of the Holy Spirit's work in us as exclusively supernatural—especially relating to the particular gifts of the Spirit—there is also much of His work that seems so natural it almost goes unnoticed. For example, the simple fact that we recognise Jesus as Lord and Saviour is a work of the Holy Spirit (1 Cor. 12:3); and that we feel convicted when we sin (John 16:8).

How likely are we to notice and thank God for this supernatural work, rather than crediting it perhaps to our own natural intellect or moral conscience? These particular works of the Spirit get easily forgotten since they seem relatively natural compared with the work of healing and prophecy, for example. God is always at work, making the supernatural seem perfectly natural to us.

Perhaps the most incredible, and yet taken-for-granted, work of the Spirit is to bring unity in the church.

I therefore, a prisoner for the Lord, urge you to walk in a manner worthy of the calling to which you have been called, with all humility and gentleness, with patience, bearing with one another in love, eager to maintain the unity of the Spirit in the bond of peace. (Eph. 4:1-3)

God enables us to feel a kindred spirit with fellow Christians. Again this is something that seems so natural that we may credit it to our own affability or good intentions. However, we should marvel at the reality of a group of people coming together—from different backgrounds, ethnicities, ages, genders, jobs, social class and neighbourhoods—and bearing with one another in a community of love. That such a community is drawn together by the work of the Spirit should be clear to us when we consider that it is more or less the opposite of how society tends to model community.

The world typically encourages us to celebrate our diversity first (as individuals) and then find our need for community fulfilled in the things we enjoy (pastimes, interests etc). However, the Spirit teaches us something very different—to recognise our equality first (as people made in the image of God) and then find diversity in our roles (in our particular place and gifting within the body of the church). As we pull together in the body we then find unity in our shared purpose and mission. So as the church, as a Spirit-filled community, we have something significant—and vital—to say about how a healthy, unified community should function. This unity may appear perfectly natural, but it isn't—it's a miraculous work of God.

We need to grasp the supernatural aspect to all these seemingly natural works of the Spirit in our lives. This assurance of God's work in our lives can then be brought into what we may consider the more extraordinary areas of church ministry. In so doing, we may treat such areas of ministry with the same comfortable balance—to see them as naturally supernatural, rather than extraordinary. To engage in them with the same confidence that we might have in peeling a potato; knowing with certainty that the Creator's divine hand is inevitably present in all that we experience.

In conclusion, both the natural and the supernatural are evident in all we experience—in every object, action and thought. The benefits of adopting this 'both-and' mindset are significant for our spiritual lives—helping us to:

1. Take childlike joy in all our experiences, even the seemingly mundane.
2. Pray more effectively, understanding earthly solutions as equally miraculous.
3. Be more open to the wider work of the Holy Spirit in our lives.
4. Continuously see the sovereignty of God in the wonder of His unfolding creation.

personal

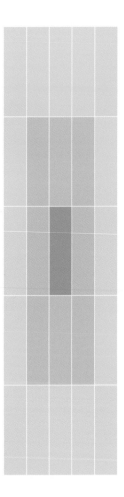

Beloved, let us love one another, for love is from God, and whoever loves has been born of God and knows God. Anyone who does not love does not know God, because God is love.

1 John 4:7-8

public

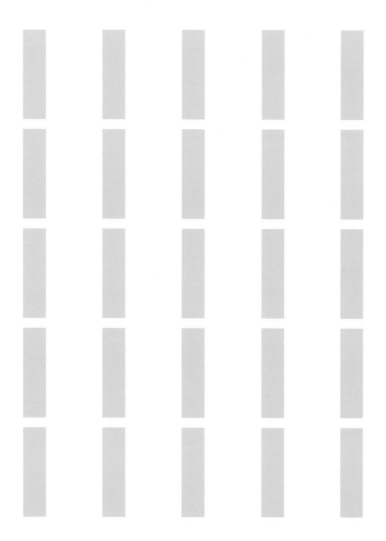

2 Timothy 3:16

All Scripture is breathed out by God and profitable for teaching, for reproof, for correction, and for training in righteousness...

personal + public

There are two different ways of 'knowing' God. He can be known to us both personally and publicly.

Personal knowledge of God occurs through direct relationship. Public knowledge, on the other hand, is information available to us without any requirement for relationship. One could argue that these two modes of knowing are not necessarily contradictory; however, we have a natural tendency to favour one over the other. We can think of the Pharisaical type who knows Scripture inside out but appears not to have the love of God in them. Conversely, many seek God's presence, who are looking for intimate spiritual connection but know nothing of the spirits they encounter. We must learn to value and cultivate both modes of knowing in order to deepen our relationship with the Lord.

But Jesus answered them, 'You are wrong, because you know neither the Scriptures nor the power of God.' (Matt. 22:29)

J.I. Packer, in *Knowing God*, explains the conviction behind his book 'is that ignorance of God—ignorance both of his ways and of the practice of communion with him—lies at the root of much of the church's weakness today'.

'Disregard the study of God,' Packer says, 'and you sentence yourself to stumble and blunder through life blindfolded, as it were, with no sense of direction and no understanding of what surrounds you. This way you can waste your life and lose your soul.'

On the other hand, as he goes on to explain: 'To be preoccupied with getting theological knowledge as an end in itself, to approach Bible study with no higher a motive than a desire to know all the answers, is the direct route to a state of self-satisfied self-deception.'

Our pursuit of informational knowledge of God, therefore, must be applied to enable our personal knowledge of Him to deepen.

At the risk of showing my age, I'm relieved to have been married before internet dating became the norm for finding relationships. We probably all know someone currently using online dating platforms. Users create a profile, which includes specific information to enable a good match with other candidates. After reading someone's profile, we could say that we know something about that candidate.

This could be defined as informational or public knowledge. If we then conducted a wider online search on the candidate, particularly via social media platforms, further public knowledge would likely be available to us. In theory, we could 'know' them better—and the more famous the person, the more public knowledge exists, the better we could 'know' them.

However, could we honestly claim to know someone—to genuinely know them—from public information alone?

In a world of fake news, coupled with the fact that most of us present heavily curated online personas, it would be especially difficult today to say we genuinely knew someone—unless, of course, we had begun to share experiences with them directly. In the same way, the public knowledge we can glean about a potential partner may help us decide whether to go on a first date, but relational knowledge only develops as experiences are shared. Thus, both informational knowing and relational knowing could be seen as necessary components to help us get to know someone more deeply.

In a sense, the Bible is God's profile to us. An important distinction to make is that God is incapable of lying. Scripture, therefore, as the authoritative Word of God, presents a reality that is not idealised or carefully curated. It's also, by contrast, a fairly comprehensive profile, giving us a very detailed picture of God. Any constructed theology we have about God is systematically derived from what is revealed through the Bible. Importantly, we are to understand Scripture as inerrant—written by man under the influence of the Spirit and, therefore, God-inspired and true.

Knowing this first of all, that no prophecy of Scripture comes from someone's own interpretation. For no prophecy was ever produced by the will of man, but men spoke from God as they were carried along by the Holy Spirit. (2 Pet. 1:20-21)

All Scripture is breathed out by God and profitable for teaching, for reproof, for correction, and for training in righteousness, that the man of God may be competent, equipped for every good work. (2 Tim. 3:16-17)

There is much to learn and grapple with in Scripture; we can know God in great detail from this comprehensive public profile. The danger is that we can spend all our time wading around gathering informational knowledge about God and never pluck up the courage to dive in and go on a first date. In other words, it's possible to know the Bible inside out, to know God's profile—to know Him 'informationally' or 'publicly'—but still not really know Him.

However, if we don't spend this valuable time in Scripture, getting to know information 'about' God, our direct relational experiences will be significantly impoverished. Just as we need to read someone's profile in order to decide what kind of date to go on; so too, our experiences with God will be more fruitful, the more we know about Him. Put simply: we can't pray effectively if we don't know the will of the Father; we can't love one another if we don't understand how God first loved us; we can't sing or write about God if we don't know how to describe His character. Scripture reveals all this information to us. I recall here the words from a sermon by Tim Keller in which he says: 'You can know your Bible and not know God, but you can't know God and not know your Bible.'

We might conclude at this point by saying that public knowledge of God through Scripture is critical to deepening our personal knowledge of God through prayer, service and worship. However, this does not entirely give us the full picture of how Scripture functions in the life of the believer.

Your word is a lamp to my feet and a light to my path. (Ps. 119:105)

As we begin to develop the rhythms of an intimate personal relationship with the Lord, we begin to read Scripture differently. The information itself changes from something public to something personal. The Word of God becomes part of our living relationship with Him. In that sense, this apparent contradiction is more than a 'both-and' scenario—it may begin as a 'both-and' scenario, but ultimately, through the work of the Holy Spirit, both sides of the equation become one. Personal and public knowledge merge, as the Bible miraculously becomes something life-giving, life-affirming and life-directing.

Another important aspect of our knowledge of God is that it is best gained through fellowship. When Philip comes across the Ethiopian reading from Isaiah (Acts chapter 8), he stops to explain the message and illuminates the gospel of Jesus through Isaiah's writing. When Thomas first misses seeing the risen Christ in the gathered community in the upper room, he is filled with doubts. Jesus does not choose to reveal Himself to Thomas until He returns to the community of believers eight days later. When Jesus appears, and Thomas touches His physical wounds, he exclaims 'My Lord and my God!' (John 20:28)—echoing the opening recognition in the book that Jesus is God.

I don't think we would be over-speculating here to conclude that the blessing of intimate knowledge of Jesus' divine personhood is revealed most profoundly in His gathered church.

In a similar sense, as we all bring individual strands of knowledge and experience of God into fellowship, it forms part of a much larger, richer tapestry, from which we may all share and grow collectively in the knowledge of the Lord.

And this is eternal life, that they know you the only true God, and Jesus Christ whom you have sent. (John 17:3)

faith

Nathanael said to him, 'Can anything good come out of Nazareth?' Philip said to him, 'Come and see.'

John 1:46

reason

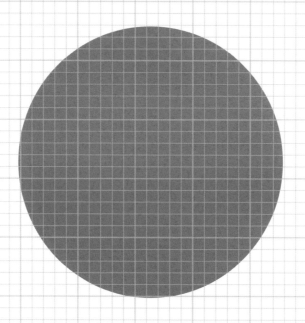

Ephesians 1:17-18

... that the God of our Lord Jesus Christ, the Father of glory, may give you a spirit of wisdom and of revelation in the knowledge of him, having the eyes of your hearts enlightened, that you may know what is the hope to which he has called you...

faith + reason

Does belief in Jesus Christ (as the crucified, resurrected Son of God) require a departure from all rational thought? Must we believe on the basis of blind faith alone?

The answer is a definitive 'no'. To understand why, we must begin by carefully defining our terms. The full range of possible relationships between the application of faith and reason in our pursuit of truth can be summarised in the following four categories: Conflicting, Distinct, Compatible and Connected.

1. Conflicting

In this model of thinking, faith is always entirely opposed to reason. Belief in God and other religious claims lies firmly in the realm of the irrational. Those who believe in God, resolving their belief by faith only, tend to be seen as religious fundamentalists. The Danish philosopher Soren Kierkegaard believed firmly in God and maintained that reason should not be employed to convince others of God's existence. 'Fideism' is the name of the extreme position at this end of the model—the conviction that belief should never be subjected to any rational justification.

At the other end of the 'conflict' model are those who would employ only reason to validate humanity's existence. This approach would be held by 'scientific naturalists', such as Richard Dawkins (though given his propensity for rhetoric, serious 'scientific naturalists' would likely distance themselves from much of his argumentation). The non-negotiable position at this end of the model is that we should only ever make conclusions about God that can be empirically proven.

2. Distinct

Within this view, there is no inherent rivalry between faith and reason because their spheres of influence do not overlap. Since they are always distinct, compartmentalisation of each is possible, and there is no necessary conflict between them—reason aims at empirical truth; religion aims at divine truths. We only choose one or other in our investigation of Christian belief.

One particular viewpoint in this model is the 'transrational' view. Both Calvin and Barth were transrationalists. They viewed religious faith as over and above reason and, therefore, believed that a position of religious belief could be arrived at purely upon self-authenticating revelation alone. Calvin prioritised the Spirit-led life as being the ultimate means through which assurance of belief was made possible.

3. Compatible

Here it is understood that there is some dialogue between faith and reason in the quest for truth. Certain aspects of religious belief are compatible with reason; other aspects, however, remain distinct and are solely matters of faith. Outside of such distinctions, any religious belief system should be able to be critically examined to evaluate whether it is coherent and without contradiction.

The compatibility view placed Christianity on firmer intellectual foundations from an early stage. Clement of Alexandria applied such thinking to clarify the creeds, using philosophical reasoning around the concepts of substance, being, and person, in order to combat heresies in the expanding church.

Augustine was a strong compatibilist, maintaining that the intellectual interrogation of religion should be understood as 'fides quaerens intellectum' (faith seeking understanding). To believe, proposed Augustine, was 'to think with assent'. Belief, therefore, required an act of the will, greater than reason alone could demand from the intellect.

Thomas Aquinas operated within a similar framework, claiming that belief consists primarily in knowledge and, therefore, is an intellectual act whose object is truth. The Catholic church follows Aquinas' general proposition that both faith and reason are essential components in the inquiry of belief.

4. Connected

This view proposes that faith and reason have an organic connection. 'Natural theology' is a form of such integrated thinking. Faith and reason are so closely related that both can work together to ratify any aspect of belief. We can either begin with proven scientific claims and build on them with related theological claims (such as the cosmological proof for God's existence). Alternatively, we can begin with theological claims and refine them with scientific thinking (for example, the argument that science would not be possible without God's intervention to make the world intelligible in the first instance).

Many philosophers and theologians hold to the possibility of 'natural theology'. Some have gone even further, attempting to unite faith and reason into a comprehensive metaphysical system where religious belief and pure rationality are in complete harmony with one another. An example of complete harmony is proposed in Immanuel Kant's *Religion within the Bounds of Bare Reason*.

Since the above summary of these four well-established categories gives only a very brief overview of each position, it may be hard to resolve which—if any—contain definitive truth. My aim here is not to attempt to convince you of a particular position but, rather, to simply propose that both faith and reason (in some form of relationship) are essential components in our belief in Christ. With that broad approach in mind, the only model of thinking that we could confidently reject as erroneous is the conflict model. The reason for this is simple: from experience, we know that we cannot confine 'reason' to the sphere of purely empirical data. John Polkinghorne, vicar and former Chair of Physics at Cambridge University, asks a simple question to demonstrate the breadth of reason (from *Science and Religion in Quest of Truth*):

'What is the reason the kettle is boiling?'

'The kettle is boiling both because gas heats the water (the scientific explanation) and because I want to make a cup of tea (an explanation invoking purpose). We do not have to choose between these two accounts, for both are true.'

We can observe from this illustration that our overall knowledge is increased by using both forms of investigation. The same is true when we question many of the claims of Christianity. We know that some degree of faith is required to resolve Christianity's more miraculous claims (those which remain outside the commonly observed order of nature). Therefore, the burden of proof rests on demonstrating that we can also utilise some element of reason to resolve its more basic claims.

That the Christian faith is witnessed in real time and history—through people, places and events—means that it presents much to investigate which is quantifiable by reasonable argument. A good example of this can be found in the investigation of Christ's resurrection. Here we can approach the historical information more forensically and use it as corroborating evidence to support the biblical claims. Books such as Frank Morrison's *Who Moved the Stone?* and Lee Strobel's *The Case for Faith* include examples of such reason-led investigation.

Another hotly debated Bible story is the creation account in Genesis. Many Christians believe that Scripture presents a theological framework that allows for an old earth interpretation. This view aligns with the scientific research of many geologists. Others argue that Genesis should be read as a straightforward historical narrative, and may advocate a younger earth interpretation. Both interpretations can be supported with some form of scientific evidence. And since faith must be required by anyone who believes that God created matter 'out of nothing' ('ex nihilo'), we can conclude that both interpretations require some combination of faith and reason to develop their respective lines of investigation.

For many, such a process of investigation is vital to ironing out personal doubts—to engage both head and heart in the pursuit of knowledge. And thankfully, this is not accomplished by our efforts alone—God acts to grant us such supernatural revelation:

… that the God of our Lord Jesus Christ, the Father of glory, may give you a spirit of wisdom and of revelation in the knowledge of him, having the eyes of your hearts enlightened, that you may know what is the hope to which he has called you… (Eph. 1:17-18)

God opens the eyes of our heart and gives us reason beyond our natural wisdom. In this, we can begin to see how faith and reason—head and heart—are inextricably linked. As French mathematician and theologian Blaise Pascal commented: 'We know the truth, not only by the reason, but also by the heart.'

To favour either faith or reason at the expense of the other has significant consequences. Without reason, we will be ill-prepared to share the gospel faithfully and, as Peter commanded:

… [to] always be prepared to make a defence to anyone who asks you for a reason for the hope that is in you... (1 Pet. 3:15)

Paul also used reason—and philosophy—to explain Christ crucified and engage the Greeks when he preached in the Areopagus. He was able to explain the gospel clearly in light of their cultural and historical reference points. Because of this rational approach, many came to believe in Christ.

On the other hand, as Calvin noted, without faith, we have no concrete assurance of our belief. In the end, the 'God-debate' will always remain philosophical until we take a leap of faith. In relationship with Christ, we experience a love that goes beyond reason.

… and to know the love of Christ that surpasses knowledge, that you may be filled with all the fullness of God. (Eph. 3:19)

When Jesus is calling the first disciples (John 1), He uses the phrase: 'come and see'. When Nathanael questions whether Jesus could be the Messiah (a few verses later), Philip replies to him with the very same phrase that Jesus used: 'come and see' (John 1:46).

The sense here in this repeated statement is that to fully understand—to believe— we have to test Christianity out in practice. Belief cannot be gained from the outside. It is not purely a theoretical matter of the mind. So too for Augustine, belief touched all the faculties—intellect, will and heart. All parts of our being must be engaged to access the knowledge and certainty of God's grace in our lives.

Do you desire to believe in Christ?

Reason may break down old arguments and open up new vistas, but only faith can help us make the final leap home.

Come and see.

3

Apparent contradictions in the characteristics of being in Christ.

sorrow + joy

wealth + poverty

weakness + strength

confidence + humility

slavery + freedom

care + abandon

saint + sinner

love + obedience

sorrow

Jesus wept.

John 11:35

joy

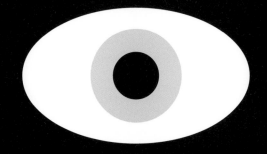

John 16:20

'Truly, truly, I say to you, you will weep and lament, but the world will rejoice. You will be sorrowful, but your sorrow will turn into joy.'

sorrow + joy

We are treated as impostors, and yet are true; ... as sorrowful, yet always rejoicing (2 Cor. 6:8-10)

Perhaps the most visible paradox in the Christian life is the tension between sorrow and joy. How is it possible that the Christian can be sorrowful yet always rejoicing? At a glance, it seems illogical that both emotions could co-exist in the present. On closer inspection, however, we can see that our sorrow and joy come from two very different sources.

Our sorrow is generally circumstantial, arising from the present suffering of this world. In communion with God in prayer, we may even share in some of His sorrow for our world. Our joy, on the other hand, comes from seeing God's kingdom triumph over our present sufferings. This joy can be part of our immediate experience, but also comes in the form of God's promise to restore this groaning creation. The Bible explains that a day is coming when our sorrow will be 'swallowed up' by our joy (John 16:20) and grief and tears will be no more (Rev. 21:4). In the meantime, as we eagerly await that day, both emotions can be understood to co-exist in tension. In adversity, we can always take hope in God's promise of restoration, which releases joy in the face of our present sorrows. In that sense, Paul's observation that we are 'sorrowful yet always rejoicing' can be understood as a simple paradox. Let's look in a little more detail at why both sorrow and joy are critical emotions in the life of the believer.

One might well imagine that the old ascetics were utterly devoid of joy. On the contrary, G.K. Chesterton argues that although they were exercising abstinence from the pleasures of this world, they were at least 'seeking' joy in the next. He compares this emphasis with the later Puritan legacy, stating that, 'the older ascetic saw heaven as very bright, and this world as dark in comparison. But the later Puritan saw heaven itself as dark, in the sense of stern and rather stormy; and his genuine imagination exulted in the storm. For him the Lord was in the thunder, much more than in the still small voice; and he was thus at the opposite extreme to even the most extreme ascetic, or excessive ascetic, who wished the sound of lutes and viols to cease, so that the still small voice might be heard. The point is, however, that the old ascetic was looking for joy and beauty, whether we think his vision of joy or beauty impossible or merely invisible. But the true Puritan was not primarily looking for joy and beauty, but for strength and even violence.'

We might well argue this statement paints a negative and unfair view of the Puritans. However, we cannot underestimate the legacy of both the ascetics and the Puritans (however confused) on the shape of the church today. While a more austere vision of faith may have dominated the twentieth century, in the last half-century, there has been a rise in new expressions of church and, in particular, seeker-sensitive churches. Regrettably, in some of this understandable backlash, the pendulum has swung too far, and we would appear to have thrown out the baby with the bathwater. A high view of God has been lost in many churches, with too much of the 'weight of God's glory' removed from sight. Where the worship of God is overtly normalised, we immediately lose something of our necessary reverence for Him. In this context, we find the caricature of the always happy, best-buddy Jesus. This trite version of Christ misses half the picture. In the fewest possible words, here's the missing part:

Jesus wept. (John 11:35)

To overcome this inevitable tension between the trite and the austere, we have created an unnecessary schism between 'joy' and 'happiness' in recent Christian language. Joy is often presented as heavenly and reverent, whereas by contrast, happiness as worldly and trite. In a culture where the pursuit of happiness seems to be the central aim for everyone, it is perhaps understandable that the church would wish to differentiate its particular pursuit of happiness. To call it 'joy' rather than 'happiness', however, makes little sense considering both words are relatively interchangeable in the Bible, and both are used regularly. The more important consideration is what the subject of our happiness or joy is: happiness or joy in God is heavenly; happiness or joy outside of God is worldly. This does not mean that we dare not, like the ascetics, find happiness in a wild flower, a relationship, a well-cooked meal... but rather that our joy in these 'good' things should point us to take joy in their ultimate source—our Creator—who provides and sustains everything.

You open your hand; you satisfy the desire of every living thing. (Ps. 145:16)

Our present joy in God is vital, and it honours our Creator. Not surprisingly, we are encouraged throughout Scripture to take joy for a wide range of reasons. James tells us to take joy in our sufferings because of the godly character it builds in us:

Count it all joy, my brothers, when you meet trials of various kinds, for you know that the testing of your faith produces steadfastness. (James 1:2-3)

In the Psalms, we are called to sing for joy to the Lord. In the process, our joy is found in our reverent awe for Him:

Clap your hands, all peoples! Shout to God with loud songs of joy! For the LORD, the Most High, is to be feared, a great king over all the earth. (Ps. 47:1-2)

We may also hope and pray for God to fill us (and our fellow believers) with joy. It is this very expression of joy that assures us of our salvation:

May the God of hope fill you with all joy and peace in believing, so that by the power of the Holy Spirit you may abound in hope. (Rom. 15:13)

Though you have not seen him, you love him. Though you do not now see him, you believe in him and rejoice with joy that is inexpressible and filled with glory, obtaining the outcome of your faith, the salvation of your souls. (1 Pet. 1:8-9)

Finally, David's plea to have the joy of salvation restored in his life, reveals one of joy's incredible functions—that our visible joy in the eternal brings other people to faith! We could perhaps need no better reason than this to tirelessly pursue our joy in Christ.

Restore to me the joy of your salvation and uphold me with a willing spirit. Then I will teach transgressors your ways and sinners will return to you. (Ps. 51:12-13)

This all-important, eternal perspective to our joy is like medicine in a broken world. When someone is thankful and joyful in God, in the face of great adversity, it is the best possible witness to God's grace. When the world sees joy and sorrow operating together in this way, Christ is most gloriously displayed in us.

So as Christians, we must be about the business of pursuing joy in Christ. But what of sorrow—should we be actively pursuing it in the same way?

Jesus was sometimes known as the 'man of sorrows' (Isa. 53:3). He grieved and often wept in His earthly life. He also suffered immeasurable pain and cruelty. It would be unnatural for us not to be sorrowful at His suffering. When we realise that we are the root cause of His suffering, it should have the impact of moving us from a state of sorrow to a state of repentance.

But he was wounded for our transgressions; he was crushed for our iniquities; upon him was the chastisement that brought us peace, and with his stripes we are healed. (Isa. 53:5)

It is precisely our grief in the Lord's suffering that compels our repentance.

For godly grief produces a repentance that leads to salvation without regret, whereas worldly grief produces death. (2 Cor. 7:10)

Notice the important distinction here between godly grief and worldly grief. For repentance to be genuine, our sorrow must come from knowing, first and foremost, that our sin is against the Lord. We see a display of godly grief from David when he seeks forgiveness after committing adultery and murder. When Nathan the prophet rebukes him, the first thing he charges David with is this:

'Why have you despised the word of the LORD, to do what is evil in his sight?' (2 Sam. 12:9)

Notice the primary concern is David's sin against God. The human casualty of the sin is not unimportant, but the reality of breaking God's Word comes first, and this is what triggers David's sorrow. This is emphasised, after his rebuke, by the first words to come out of David's lips:

David said to Nathan, 'I have sinned against the LORD.' (2 Sam. 12:13)

This response reveals David's view of the primacy of God. God comes first, and the sorrow that comes from breaking His law is what leads to genuine repentance. In this state, David actively pursues forgiveness and asks God to remove his sorrow and restore him to a state of joy (Psalm 51).

In that sense, our sorrow is something we should aim to move on from by the grace of God. Dwelling for too long in a place of sorrow can easily foster a sense of hopelessness. Although sorrow is not considered a virtue, we are called to a state of sorrow for those who mourn:

Rejoice with those who rejoice, weep with those who weep. (Rom. 12:15)

Sorrow is, therefore, a right and natural response to both the suffering of Christ and to our present broken world. It is the birthplace of our repentance, and of our compassion for this world. In sorrow, we are driven to pray for God's kingdom to come in fullness and for every tear to be wiped away. The Bible assures us this day is coming:

He will wipe away every tear from their eyes, and death shall be no more, neither shall there be mourning, nor crying, nor pain any more, for the former things have passed away. (Rev. 21:4)

Scripture also presents us with the great news that not only will there be an end to sorrow, but our sorrow will actually be transformed into joy:

'Truly, truly, I say to you, you will weep and lament, but the world will rejoice. You will be sorrowful, but your sorrow will turn into joy.' (John 16:20)

He will swallow up death forever; and the LORD God will wipe away tears from all faces, and the reproach of his people he will take away from all the earth, for the LORD has spoken. It will be said on that day, 'Behold, this is our God; we have waited for him, that he might save us. This is the LORD; we have waited for him; let us be glad and rejoice in his salvation.' (Isaiah 25:8-9)

wealth

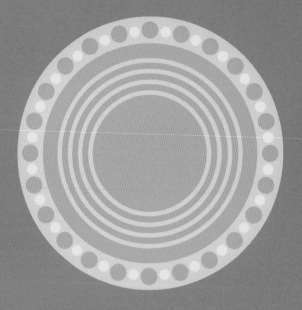

'For you know the grace of our Lord Jesus Christ, that   2 Corinthians 8:9
though he was rich, yet for your sake he became poor, so
that you by his poverty might become rich.'

poverty

'Blessed are the poor in spirit, for theirs is the kingdom of heaven.'

wealth + poverty

There is a huge problem in the church today with 'prosperity gospel' teaching. Manipulative leaders focus on the potential material wealth that God has in store for us today, often suggesting certain behaviours and practices that might unlock the floodgates of some heavenly slot machine. And yet, in the Bible, we see no such promises. If anything the picture is the reverse, with Scripture revealing that—in this life—Christians can expect tribulation (Acts 14:22), suffering (Rom. 8:17), and persecution (2 Tim. 3:12). Furthermore, the teaching throughout the New Testament, especially by Jesus, seems to favour the poor over the prosperous.

'It is easier for a camel to go through the eye of a needle than for a rich person to enter the kingdom of God.' (Mark 10:25)

While we can never conclude from Scripture that wealth and poverty presents an 'either-or' scenario for kingdom access, there is undoubtedly a greater focus in the New Testament on the danger of material riches. This bias towards the poor could be understood in several ways: firstly, that the poor are sometimes empathetically favoured due to the injustice and hardship of their poverty; secondly, that the poverty itself could be counted as a blessing—since it causes the necessary dependence and desperation to cry out to God for deliverance; and thirdly, as a counter-balance to the oversimplified line of thought at the time, which held that material wealth was a blessing from God, while poverty was a curse.

The Jews would have looked back and noted the significant material wealth of many of the great figures in their history, such as Job (Job 1:3), David (1 Chron. 22:14) and Solomon (2 Chron. 9:13). Since separation from God had often resulted in exile, persecution and financial hardship for the Israelites, it's perhaps easy to see why they viewed material poverty as a curse or punishment. In contrast to this picture, of course, Jesus lived in relative poverty, and the Apostles were not materially wealthy, sharing and giving away all they owned.

Despite this apparent New Testament disposition towards material poverty, we can observe that Joseph of Arimathea was said to have great material wealth. The reverse is also true—it was not all temples and riches in the Old Testament—Moses gave up on the vast material wealth available to him in Egypt to follow God's call. Furthermore, the Bible never presents poverty as a virtue—even making clear that poverty can be sinful and self-inflicted:

Slothfulness casts into a deep sleep, and an idle person will suffer hunger. (Prov. 19:15)

It's also true, by contrast, that if we honour our God-given talents and our mandate to work, material wealth could be a likely outcome. Many successful and well-established businesses in Western society are both founded on, and operating with, Christian values—even if unintentionally.

Applying a broader brush, we could ascertain that Scripture does not allow us to create any neat categories about the benefits of either material wealth or poverty. The book of Proverbs suggests a more level playing field:

Rich and poor have this in common: The LORD is the Maker of them all. (Prov. 22:2 NIV)

Proverbs also provides an incredibly helpful measuring of the dangers of both poverty and riches:

… give me neither poverty nor riches; feed me with the food that is needful for me, lest I be full and deny you and say, 'Who is the LORD?' or lest I be poor and steal and profane the name of my God. (Prov. 30:8-9)

The Apostle Paul gives us a similarly pragmatic summary of circumstantial wealth:

Not that I am speaking of being in need, for I have learned in whatever situation I am to be content. I know how to be brought low, and I know how to abound. In any and every circumstance, I have learned the secret of facing plenty and hunger, abundance and need. (Phil. 4:11-12)

In summary, we could say that our level of material wealth should have no bearing in an eternal sense, as long as we are mindful of the potential dangers we face in either extreme. Our concern should be that in abundance, we don't create a foothold for pride or greed; just as in lack, we don't create a foothold for envy or despondency. Therefore, of significantly more importance than being rich or poor, is the condition of our heart in either state. In that sense, the Bible primarily calls us to question our spiritual wealth.

It's interesting that in Luke's account of the beatitudes, he simply recounts the line: 'Blessed are the poor.' Jump to Matthew's account, however, and he qualifies this as 'Blessed are the poor in spirit':

'Blessed are the poor in spirit, for theirs is the kingdom of heaven.' (Matt. 5:3)

Luke, a doctor, may simply have been giving us a more earthly perspective here. Matthew, however, drills into the spiritual aspect of our wealth. It's important to note this distinction, because, where we might conclude that our level of material wealth doesn't matter (at least, outside of extreme poverty); our level of spiritual wealth does matter. Our conclusion should no longer be an either-or scenario. It matters that we are both rich and poor in a spiritual sense.

But how is it possible to be both spiritually rich and spiritually poor?

Matthew records Jesus' incredible claim that the poor in spirit qualify to receive the richest spiritual blessing of all—the kingdom of heaven. The reason for this? Because being spiritually poor requires us to recognise our need for God; to recognise that because of sin, God's help is required to deliver us. Therefore to inherit the kingdom, to be spiritually wealthy, paradoxically, comes from first recognising our spiritual poverty.

When we recognise our spiritual poverty, we depend on Christ, who by His poverty makes us rich.

For you know the grace of our Lord Jesus Christ, that though he was rich, yet for your sake he became poor, so that you by his poverty might become rich. (2 Cor. 8:9)

In conclusion, the biblical paradox of having both wealth and poverty can be explained simply as our need to be poor enough in spirit to recognise our dependence on God. In that faithful dependence, we become spiritually rich through the great inheritance He has provided us. This exchange provides an amazing truth: we have a God who so limited and impoverished Himself, even to death on a cross, that the wealth of salvation, the riches of heaven, were made available to us by faith in Him.

How greatly we need to value these spiritual riches in heaven, over and above any form of present material wealth! And should we be fortunate enough to have gained material wealth, our posture should be to share our wealth generously with those in need, whom God has given us to look after. The incredible benefit of such generosity is to be blessed directly by God:

Whoever is generous to the poor lends to the LORD, and he will repay him for his deed. (Prov. 19:17)

weakness

———

But he said to me, 'My grace is sufficient for you, for my power is made perfect in weakness.' Therefore I will boast all the more gladly of my weaknesses, so that the power of Christ may rest upon me.

2 Corinthians 12:9

strength

2 Corinthians 12:10

For the sake of Christ, then, I am content with weaknesses, insults, hardships, persecutions, and calamities. For when I am weak, then I am strong.

weakness + strength

—————

Writing to the church in Corinth, Paul makes the surprising statement: 'For when I am weak, then I am strong.' Read in isolation this seems to present an impossible conflict: how could anyone display both weakness and strength at the same time? When we consider the surrounding context, however, we can observe that both the source of weakness and the source of strength, come from two very different places.

But he said to me, 'My grace is sufficient for you, for my power is made perfect in weakness.' Therefore I will boast all the more gladly of my weaknesses, so that the power of Christ may rest upon me. For the sake of Christ, then, I am content with weaknesses, insults, hardships, persecutions, and calamities. For when I am weak, then I am strong. (2 Cor. 12:9-10)

Notice that the strength—the power—comes from God. The weakness comes from Paul. The various weaknesses Paul lists here could be understood better as his limitations. In other words, they are the things outside his control that befall him—the things he must bear, as opposed to any sinful actions he himself might make. The specific weakness Paul describes earlier in this passage as his 'thorn in the flesh' is never revealed in any more detail. He appears to have had some significant hindrance throughout his ministry, which may well have been a physical weakness. Paul even prays for it to be removed, but eventually acknowledges that God uses this weakness to display His strength more visibly through Paul. He also, perhaps even more surprisingly, acknowledges that God imposes this particular limitation on him. Such was Paul's awareness of the danger of pride in his life that he understood the benefit of this imposition.

Like a nail hammered into wood, as the thorn went deeper into Paul's side, so Paul drove himself deeper into Christ. His reliance on God increased and his self-sufficiency—his pride—was axed at the root. Paul, being firmly in Christ, was therefore strengthened by God's hand to enable him to cope with pain, imprisonment and all manner of hardship. His character was refined through this process, as he placed his trust in the sufficiency of God's grace and might.

Joy is what we should express when we consider our own thorn in the flesh: that because of it, we can register our weakness and look to Christ for His sustaining strength. Matthew Henry's commentary on this passage notes helpfully, 'when we feel that we are weak in ourselves, then we go to Christ, receive strength from him and enjoy most the supplies of Divine strength and grace.'

This is arguably a paradox that is easy to explain in theory, but hard to enact in practice. How many of us desire to think of ourselves as 'weak', especially in a culture where we have become increasingly self-sufficient? In the well-educated, financially stable ranks of society, all our immediate daily needs—shelter, food, protection, community—are met without apparent need or reliance on anyone except ourselves. The more complex and automated the system of provision around us, the less apparent is God's provision behind it all.

We trust so much in our own strength today; and yet, all it takes is a financial crash or a viral pandemic, and the rug is abruptly pulled from under us. We quickly realise that we were never really in control of our own lives. These disasters that befall us corporately as nations should have the same effect as the weaknesses that befall us as individuals. When things crumble and fall apart, our reliance must be placed again on a mighty God—a God who can step in and rebuild with strong foundations—a God who has the limitless power to increase our strength, even at our weakest.

Have you not known? Have you not heard? The LORD is the everlasting God, the Creator of the ends of the earth. He does not faint or grow weary; his understanding is unsearchable. He gives power to the faint, and to him who has no might he increases strength. Even youths shall faint and be weary, and young men shall fall exhausted; but they who wait for the LORD shall renew their strength; they shall mount up with wings like eagles; they shall run and not be weary; they shall walk and not faint. (Isa. 40:28-31)

As individuals, and as nations, Isaiah reminds us of our fallibility and our resulting need for God's sustaining strength. In the story of the Tower of Babel (Gen. 11), our corporate fallibility is made plain—we learn that no matter how advanced humanity becomes, we cannot reach heaven in our own strength. A Messiah would be required to bridge the gap. In our human weakness, we would only reach heaven by God's strength. Salvation comes from the Lord, from Christ crucified. And it is precisely by His crucifixion, that Jesus gives us the perfect model of strength in apparent weakness.

At the time, the Jews expected their Messiah to be a mighty warrior-king. Military strength was their chief expectation of Jesus. They were ill-prepared for their Messiah to display such apparent weakness as to be captured, tortured and crucified by human hand—to be put to death in the most humiliating way.

It is also this display of apparent weakness that remains a barrier to faith in Christ for many today. Muslims, in particular, identify with Jesus as a prophet but struggle to accept that a prophet could be humiliated on a cross. Resulting theories exist which speculate that Jesus was not crucified at all. Some suggest a case of mistaken identity in Jesus' arrest at the Garden of Gethsemane. But for the Christian, there is no greater potion—no greater strength than taking Christ's suffering into our very core being.

Charles Spurgeon quotes one of the early martyrs as saying, 'I can bear it all, for Jesus suffered, and he suffers in me now; he sympathises with me, and this makes me strong.'

Paradoxically then, it is when we register our weakness and cleave to the grace of the Lord, that His strength is made visible through us; a strength which itself was made manifest out of His apparent weakness—His suffering on the cross.

confidence

Do not be afraid of sudden terror or of the ruin of the wicked, when it comes, for the LORD will be your confidence and will keep your foot from being caught.

Proverbs 3:25-26

humility

———

Isaiah 6:5

*'Woe is me! For I am lost; for I am a man of unclean lips, and I dwell in the midst of a people of unclean lips; for my eyes have seen the King, the L*ORD *of hosts!'*

confidence + humility

Confidence and humility may well appear to be contradictory. We might assume that where a confident person will put themself forward, a humble person will instead play themself down. I would argue, however, that confidence and humility are not contradictory at all. They only appear in opposition because we've lost sense of the original meaning of the word 'humility'. There is a tendency today to think of humility as something more akin to what we ought to call 'false humility', or 'obsequiousness'. In other words, humility is only expressed when we put ourselves down or falsely exaggerate our lack of worth. It's easy then to see how this wrong view of humility is the opposite of confidence. Even some dictionary definitions compound this wrong-thinking, explaining humility as a low self-regard and sense of unworthiness. This culturally ingrained notion of 'thinking lowly of oneself', however, has little to do with the original meaning of humility.

We get our word 'humility' from the Latin word 'humilitas', a noun related to the adjective 'humilis', which can be translated as 'humble' and also as 'grounded' or 'from the earth'. It derives from the Latin word 'humus', meaning 'ground', or more specifically, the layer in the soil that is teeming with life. In that sense, to be human (from the Latin word 'humanus') means to be 'a man of the ground'. Not surprisingly, the same close relationship between the concepts of man and ground also appears in the Hebrew, where the word for man is 'Adam' and the word for ground is 'adamah'. In precisely the same sense, 'Adam' could be translated as 'the ground man'; or, 'the man who was made from the ground'. Both these Hebrew and Latin roots, of course, find their genesis in the biblical account of man's creation.

Then the LORD God formed a man from the dust of the ground and breathed into his nostrils the breath of life, and the man became a living being. (Gen. 2:7)

As human beings, we were made from the ground by the breath of God. As such, our connection to both God and earth is profound. To show humility, then, is simply to recognise our place in God's creation—to remember that He made us from the ground, and we are dependent on Him for life.

With that definition in mind, we might well ask the question: how can humility make sense outside of God? The simple answer is: it doesn't. And yet, even in Christian circles today, we often see humility defined with little reference to God. Many Christians have paraphrased a definition of humility that sounds something like this: 'humility is not thinking less of yourself, but thinking of yourself less.' This definition may well have derived from a passage found in *Mere Christianity*, where

C.S. Lewis writes, regarding the truly humble man: 'He will not be thinking about humility: he will not be thinking about himself at all.'

There is, of course, some truth in this statement, and it does helpfully guard us against the misconception of false humility. However, in isolation, it bears no reference to God. Imagine a teenage boy playing intently on an X-box. He's likely to be so caught up in the activity of gaming that he won't be thinking about himself at all. At the same time, it would be hard to argue that he's expressing any genuine humility in the process.

Humility, by definition, does require us to think about ourselves. It requires us to think about ourselves in relation to God—to know our place. Isaiah comes undone in the presence of God, not because he is avoiding thinking of himself; but precisely because he is thinking of himself—realising his sin in relation to a completely holy God. His iniquities are brought to light against the weight of God's holiness:

'Woe is me! For I am lost; for I am a man of unclean lips, and I dwell in the midst of a people of unclean lips; for my eyes have seen the King, the LORD of hosts!' (Isa. 6:5)

As with Isaiah, humility initially leads to despair when we acknowledge God's right to be angered at our corrupted nature. Thankfully this is not the final picture of humility—just the starting point—God, in His mercy, does not leave us in despair. If the humble person falls to their knees, understanding their iniquities in relation to God's holiness, God is quick to restore their broken relationship:

… if my people who are called by my name humble themselves, and pray and seek my face and turn from their wicked ways, then I will hear from heaven and will forgive their sin and heal their land. (2 Chron. 7:14)

Since humility is always defined by our relationship to God, our expression of humility changes when God redeems us. Isaiah realises the chasm between himself and God and is in despair. He duly falls on his face before the Lord. God then lifts him up and places him back on his feet—it is a work of the Lord that gives Isaiah the confidence to stand.

In Isaiah chapter 9, Isaiah receives a revelation that the coming Messiah will eventually bridge the chasm between God and us. This promise of a restored relationship with the Creator moves Isaiah from despair to confidence. In that sense, through salvation, confidence is the natural endpoint and high expression of our humility. Standing in the sure foundation of Christ, knowing that our Creator has set His approval and love on us—even at so great a cost to Himself—should fill us with incredible confidence.

This truth brings us to the simple conclusion that confidence and humility are not contradictory, but rather, are two sides of the same coin. Only when we humble ourselves as 'people of the ground'—made in God's image but having fallen short of His glory—can we stand before God and confidently receive His mercy. And only when our humility points us to the sure foundation of Christ, that He treasured us enough to die for us, will we have genuine, unshakeable confidence—a confidence that comes from Him alone.

For the LORD will be your confidence and will keep your foot from being caught. (Prov. 3:26)

slavery

————

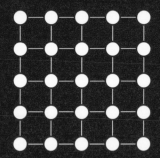

For when you were slaves of sin, you were free in regard to righteousness. But what fruit were you getting at that time from the things of which you are now ashamed? For the end of those things is death.

Romans 6:20-21

freedom

Galatians 5:13

For you were called to freedom, brothers. Only do not use your freedom as an opportunity for the flesh, but through love serve one another.

slavery + freedom

The secular person might well assume they possess a great deal more freedom than the religious person. Religion is, after all, dominated by rules and rituals. To adhere to them requires discipline and hard work. So it would seem logical that dedicated service in any religion requires time, energy and focus. Coupled to this, the world view of the religious person must, by necessity, move towards something more specific, something narrower. All this naturally serves to create the perception of diminishing freedom and choice.

In more recent history, some apologists have argued the case that Christianity is distinctly non-religious—at least in the sense that it is primarily a relationship rather than a rule-book. However, we cannot escape the reality of discipline and service required in the Christian life. And since Christian service is primarily God-centred—rather than self-centred—this appears only to inhibit freedom further. The very language Paul uses takes this idea of God-centeredness to an extreme conclusion, referring to Christians as 'slaves to Christ'.

For he who was called in the Lord as a slave is a freedman of the Lord. Likewise he who was free when called is a slave of Christ. (1 Cor. 7:22)

So how can the person who serves God, who is a slave to Christ, possibly have any freedom? Surely the path to freedom is more likely found in the person outside of faith, with no rules and no higher 'other' requiring accountability? Scripture reveals the surprising conclusion that freedom is found only in Christ. The simple reason is that, outside of Christ, everyone is naturally a slave to sin. Although that position might initially appear to offer freedom, Paul describes it as a fruitless endeavour:

For when you were slaves of sin, you were free in regard to righteousness. But what fruit were you getting at that time from the things of which you are now ashamed? For the end of those things is death. (Rom. 6:20-21)

The sobering conclusion Paul leaves us with is that anyone outside of Christ is not only a slave to sin, but is bound for destruction as a result. This process may not seem immediately evident to us, for two reasons: firstly, as the Bible explains, we are blinded to sin's grip on our lives (2 Cor. 4:4); and secondly, sin tends to enslave us over time. Although I would neither undertake nor recommend experimentation, some would maintain that you can boil a frog by placing it in cold water and very slowly bringing the water to boil. If you place the frog straight into boiling water, however, it will immediately jump out. The former process may help us understand how sin enslaves and ultimately destroys us without our even noticing.

In order to get the right biblical perspective, we need to understand a few things about the nature of sin and hell. The Bible explains that God and sin simply cannot co-exist (Ps. 5:4). Therefore, when we sin, we make an active choice to turn our backs on God—to be apart from Him. Hell, as both the active judgement of God and the inevitable conclusion to a life of sin, is simply being outside of God's blessing for all eternity. What starts with the freedom of will to turn our backs on God, quickly develops into patterns of sin that so grip us—so enslave us—that there is eventually no will left to choose God's mercy.

This process can be best understood in the context of addiction. Alcohol, drugs, gambling, pornography—whatever the poison—it all works in the same way: the user needs more and more of the substance to get the same high as before. This increased loading puts a destructive strain on the addict—like a fire that demands more and more of the soul until eventually, there is nothing of the person left.

Sheol, the barren womb, the land never satisfied with water, and the fire that never says, 'Enough.' (Prov. 30:16)

Anyone who has been through the terrible process of addiction, or seen it first hand, will know the grip it has on people's lives. Sin enslaves a person in broadly the same way as addiction. It destroys and dehumanises the captive over time, leaving the soul so charred and twisted that complete isolation—hell—is the only conclusion.

Maybe in our short lifetime, we imagine that we have a handle on our pride; on our lust; on our anger; on our greed… maybe it's only getting very mildly worse in our lifetime. But imagine it getting worse over all eternity.

In *Mere Christianity*, C.S. Lewis explains the process like this: 'Christianity asserts that every individual human being is going to live for ever, and this must be either true or false. Now there are a good many things which would not be worth bothering about if I were going to live only seventy years, but which I had better bother about very seriously if I am going to live for ever. Perhaps my bad temper or my jealousy are gradually getting worse—so gradually that the increase in seventy years will not be very noticeable. But it might be absolute hell in a million years: in fact, if Christianity is true, hell is the precisely correct technical term for what it would be.'

Sin grips us over time, like a coiling snake, with slow muscular inevitability. It squeezes our will and identity from us and eventually locks us in hell—in bondage and decay—the ultimate loss of freedom. C.S. Lewis again, in *The Problem of Pain*, paints the picture that those in hell will 'enjoy forever the horrible freedom they have demanded, and are therefore self-enslaved: just as the blessed, forever submitting to obedience, become through all eternity more and more free.'

Frightening as this should be to us, the good news is that we have a mighty God—a redeemer who can unlock any chains:

Is not this the fast that I choose: to loose the bonds of wickedness, to undo the straps of the yoke, to let the oppressed go free, and to break every yoke? (Isa. 58:6)

In the context of sin as addiction, this freedom could be understood as God rewiring us. Physiologically speaking, new neural pathways are formed in the brain as an addiction develops. This development occurs as the addictive process chemically alters the brain's communication system. When the addictive substance is removed, the brain has to form new neural pathways. This process of renewal is painful—like growing new muscles and learning to walk again after a severe physical accident.

Do not be conformed to this world, but be transformed by the renewal of your mind, that by testing you may discern what is the will of God, what is good and acceptable and perfect. (Rom. 12:2)

In God's economy, the transformation of the mind is possible; and, by the grace of God, anyone who discerns the Father's will can be renewed:

But thanks be to God, that you who were once slaves of sin have become obedient from the heart to the standard of teaching to which you were committed, and, having been set free from sin, have become slaves of righteousness. (Rom. 6:17-18)

So by God's grace, we are no longer slaves to sin; instead, we are slaves to Christ. But how does being a slave to Christ increase our freedom—aren't there still a load of rules? Well, freedom, ironically, doesn't come from the absence of rules. A helpful analogy might be to imagine if someone wanted to become a great concert pianist. They would need to discipline their life with hours of training and practice. However, when they perfect their art—when they've persevered through all the training sessions, and all the hard work is done—then they're effectively freed up to create and play the most amazing music. So, ironically, without the many hours of service towards the goal of making music, there is limited ability to perform the task with any real freedom. The same is true of anything worthwhile—genuine freedom arrives through discipline. Freedom in the Christian life grows through obedient service to Christ.

I will always obey your law, for ever and ever. I will walk about in freedom, for I have sought out your precepts. (Ps. 119:44-45 NIV)

In that sense, Christ is like the framework we operate in or the air we breathe. He is the purpose for which we were made. Like the well-known analogy, a fish is most free in water because it's designed to breathe in water—designed perfectly for its apparent constraint.

'Take my yoke upon you, and learn from me, for I am gentle and lowly in heart, and you will find rest for your souls. For my yoke is easy, and my burden is light.' (Matt. 11:29-30)

So paradoxically, being a slave to Christ, putting on His yoke in obedient service, gives us the freedom to find rest for our souls. In sharp contrast, the apparent freedom offered by the world leads to patterns of sin that will enslave our souls forever.

For freedom Christ has set us free; stand firm therefore, and do not submit again to a yoke of slavery. (Gal. 5:1)

care

But seek the welfare of the city where I have sent you
into exile, and pray to the LORD on its behalf, for in its
welfare you will find your welfare.

Jeremiah 29:7

abandon

Genesis 3:17-18

... cursed is the ground because of you; in pain you shall eat of it all the days of your life; thorns and thistles it shall bring forth for you...

care + abandon

Like a low-squatting sumo wrestler, shifting his weight from leg to leg, we straddle the kingdoms of heaven and earth. One foot in this world and one in the next. As we look forward with hope to our future dwelling with God, how should we understand our relationship with our current environment?

For we know that the whole creation has been groaning together in the pains of childbirth until now. (Rom. 8:22)

Is this groaning world, which Paul tells us has been 'subjected to futility' (Rom. 8:20), worth our concern and care? Or is it some temporary prison to be fled and abandoned?

Eastern philosophy often reveals the purpose of religion as a means of escape from our physical environment. There is less emphasis on being actively resident in the world, which is seen merely as a passing affliction. Tarnished by pain and suffering, the goal, through religious practice, is to elevate oneself to some higher spiritual plane of enlightenment, or nirvana, where physical pain and suffering are no more. Regrettably, many Christians understand heaven in approximately the same way— as an escape hatch from the drudgery and futility of our corrupted world.

In 1966, Christian and historian Lynn White, delivered an address to the American Association for the Advancement of Science, in which he aimed to highlight an error in a particular strain of Christian thinking. As a result of the widespread misunderstanding of Genesis 1:26, White's view was that Christianity 'bears a huge burden of guilt for the devastation of nature in which the West has been engaged for centuries.'

Then God said, 'Let us make man in our image, after our likeness. And let them have dominion over the fish of the sea and over the birds of the heavens and over the livestock and over all the earth and over every creeping thing that creeps on the earth.' (Gen. 1:26)

The two key points of confusion that White noted were centred around an over-emphasis of our importance in creation. Firstly, that because of the distinction made between man (formed specifically in God's image) and the rest of the created order, we have aligned ourselves more closely to God—or even *as* God—and adopted a human-centred view of His creation. Secondly, we tend to read man's 'dominion' over nature with a more worldly and sinful sense of the concept of authority. We only need to glance at our human efforts to self-govern to see how easily we misuse power. White argues that this wrong thinking has placed humanity in a privileged and reckless position over the rest of creation. Thus, Judeo-Christian thinking has cultivated a dispassionate view of nature, which has spread throughout Western society in general.

Of course, this is not the view held by many Christians; and it would be difficult to determine exactly how influential this confused line of thinking has been on society's view of the environment over the course of history. Thankfully, in Christian teaching today, much of the wrong thinking on this matter has already been addressed. Our current environmental concerns have forced a much-needed re-evaluation of the Christian's relationship to nature. The kind of human-centred thinking that Lynn White highlighted is, of course, not what we should understand from Scripture. From start to finish, the Bible teaches us something very different about our place in creation.

In the beginning, humanity was given a clear mandate to care for creation (Gen. 2:15). To Adam was given the job of cultivating the ground and of naming every species (Gen. 2:19). With these responsibilities, science and agriculture were birthed, enabling us to become more effective caretakers of God's creation. Shortly after that commissioning, we witness things going quickly downhill, as humanity falls from grace and chooses self over God. At this critical turning point in history, corruption enters the world and all of creation is said to be marred by sin's presence:

'Cursed is the ground because of you; through painful toil you will eat food from it all the days of your life. It will produce thorns and thistles for you, and you will eat the plants of the field.'
(Gen. 3:17-18)

From this, we must first understand that nature has been marred or made imperfect by our broken relationship with our Creator. In other words, we are the problem! Like a tiny cog in a watch, turning on the wrong axis, our sin has affected the entire system. The rest of creation is grinding and groaning against the tarnished element. The problem cog—humanity—nearly came to an abrupt end in the days of Noah. The Bible reveals how corrupt the human heart had become. Nearly all of humanity had turned away from their Creator. In those days, God came perilously close to destroying all of creation with a flood. Instead, what we witness after the waters subside is God's promise to save creation from our selfishness. The rainbow is the sign of His protection:

'I will remember my covenant that is between me and you and every living creature of all flesh. And the waters shall never again become a flood to destroy all flesh. When the bow is in the clouds, I will see it and remember the everlasting covenant between God and every living creature of all flesh

that is on the earth.' God said to Noah, 'This is the sign of the covenant that I have established between me and all flesh that is on the earth.' (Gen. 9:15-17)

As God's restoration plan comes into sharper view in the New Testament, we see that not only does God promise to protect creation from humanity, He also promises to restore it for His redeemed people. As Paul explains:

... the creation itself will be set free from its bondage to corruption and obtain the freedom of the glory of the children of God. (Rom. 8:21)

This incredible plan is then revealed in more detail at the very end of the Bible. In Revelation, we read that the future promise of God is not that we go up to heaven to leave this physical world behind, but instead, that a new heaven and new earth are to come down to us.

The creation is to be redeemed, therefore, in a similar way to our physical bodies—renewed rather than completely replaced—a swallowing up of our mortality (2 Cor. 5:4). God has planned from the beginning a physical and spiritual restoration job on the largest imaginable scale:

Then I saw a new heaven and a new earth, for the first heaven and the first earth had passed away, and the sea was no more. And I saw the holy city, new Jerusalem, coming down out of heaven from God, prepared as a bride adorned for her husband. And I heard a loud voice from the throne saying, 'Behold, the dwelling place of God is with man. He will dwell with them, and they will be his people, and God himself will be with them as their God.' (Rev. 21:1-3)

That God will renew—rather than replace—this groaning creation should give us all the motive we need to be fully invested in this world. What was broken is not yet lost, what was marred by sin is not beyond hope, and what God will one day redeem we must continue to care for. God originally made His creation good, and although we have subjected it to decay, He plans to protect and restore it. For this reason, we must endeavour to fulfil our initial God-given role as caretakers of creation; to be fully resident, despite the deserved hardships—despite the thorns and thistles.

Irrespective of this powerful motive for our active care and curation in the world, it's also perfectly natural for us to feel alien in it. In all of creation, in the human heart most notably, we see plainly the effects of sin, and we understandably long to detach ourselves from that influence. Jesus understood this tension. Scripture clearly warns us not to love this world (James 4:4) or to be 'conformed' by the things of this world (Rom. 12:2).

Do not love the world or the things in the world. If anyone loves the world, the love of the Father is not in him. (1 John 2:15)

In all these instances, however, we should note the distinction between 'the creation' and 'the world'. The commentaries on these verses explain the meaning of 'world' as being the prevailing wicked habits of the current culture. It is this wickedness that the Christian is called to be in opposition with—to resist any cultural behaviour that is not in accordance with the will of God. This is the 'world' that we must be careful to align ourselves with too closely. By contrast, we are nowhere given the command to abandon 'the creation'. Instead, as Christ Himself did, we are called to step into the mess, to take residency in this broken world and seek the welfare of the environment we find ourselves in.

But seek the welfare of the city where I have sent you into exile, and pray to the LORD on its behalf, for in its welfare you will find your welfare. (Jer. 29:7)

We are called as the church to do this. Not just for our environment, but for the people living therein. We are to have love and empathy for all God's creation—to see everyone and everything with inherent value, as being made by God; and therefore with the potential to be renewed by God—to become, as yet not fully known, part of our future dwelling and inheritance.

saint

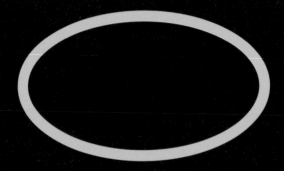

To the church of God that is in Corinth, to those
sanctified in Christ Jesus, called to be saints together
with all those who in every place call upon the name of
our Lord Jesus Christ.

1 Corinthians 1:2

sinner

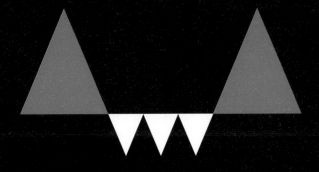

---

1 John 1:8   *If we say we have no sin, we deceive ourselves, and the*
                               truth is not in us.

saint + sinner

Do you think of yourself more as a 'saint' or a 'sinner'? The extraordinary picture, presented by the Bible, is that we are both. Those who are in Christ are revealed as both saint and sinner at the same time.

Martin Luther coined this state of tension as: 'Simul Iustus et Peccator', meaning, 'At the same time, justified and sinners'.

The way this works is that when we are justified by Christ, we become saints by position. All who believe and belong to the body of Christ are defined in the New Testament as 'hagios', which is the word for a saint. 'Hagios' can be translated as sacred, pure, blameless, holy, set apart. Hence, when we are made right by Christ's work on the cross, we are set apart for salvation as a body of believing saints. This is what it means to be called a saint: to inherit holiness, to be treated as blameless because we are protected in Christ.

To the church of God that is in Corinth, to those sanctified in Christ Jesus, called to be saints together with all those who in every place call upon the name of our Lord Jesus Christ. (1 Cor. 1:2)

It would, therefore, be important to see that we are saints only by our God-given position—through our trust in Christ's work alone. Our good deeds do not qualify us for sainthood. Nevertheless, there is much confusion with this notion. We often hear of a secular person being referred to as a saint, perhaps on account of their good deeds in society. Strictly speaking, this branding widens the net too much, since, by definition, we are only saints on account of our justification by faith in Christ. The Roman Catholic position, on the other hand, tightens the net—only those canonised after death by the Pope are recognised as saints. The language used in the early church, however, defined the entire body of believers as saints, whether living or dead:

Now as Peter went here and there among them all, he came down also to the saints who lived at Lydda. (Acts 9:32)

All the saints greet you, especially those of Caesar's household. (Phil. 4:22)

So, Scripture reveals that we are saints by being in Christ and belonging to His church. To what extent, then, should we also understand ourselves as sinners? G.K. Chesterton made the well-known quip that the greatest single argument against Christianity is Christians! Regrettably, this is often true. How many times have we heard an argument like this: 'What good is Christianity? The only Christians I know are hypocrites.'

We need to be ready to put our hands up as Christians and confess that our behaviour is often worse than the many people living morally upright lives in the world around us. The main reason for this contradiction is simple. Glorification is not an overnight process. As Christians, we recognise our brokenness and are dependent on God to be changed as we walk in obedience, in step with the Spirit. During this process, we remain sinners until Jesus returns to complete the good work He began in us. Thus all professing Christians can be seen to sin. Another category exists, of course, that many professing Christians are not genuine in their faith and, as such, have no process of sanctification at work in their lives (Matt. 7:21).

But whether morally upright or not, or whether authentically saved or not, Romans 3:23 explains that all have sinned and fall short of the glory of God. Every human being has inherited sin from the point at which Adam disobeyed God and chose self over God. Therefore nobody can make an excuse for sin. So how are the saints in Christ to deal with the pervasive nature of sin in their lives? The book of 1 John provides a very helpful guide for the believer. The disciple John, talking specifically to Christians, begins by explaining the reality that sin exists in the life of a saint, even after coming to faith:

If we say we have no sin, we deceive ourselves, and the truth is not in us. (1 John 1:8)

As saints, we need to be aware of the immense spiritual battle going on around us when we come to faith in Jesus. Outside of faith, we have no real enemies. Our enmity is only with God. However fearful we ought to be of so great an adversary, the truth remains that God desires for each one of us to be reconciled to Him. At the point of conversion, however, the believer gains a new ally in God but creates three distinct enemies. The Bible describes these as the world, the flesh and the devil:

And you were dead in the trespasses and sins in which you once walked, following the course of this world, following the prince of the power of the air, the spirit that is now at work in the sons of disobedience—among whom we all once lived in the passions of our flesh, carrying out the desires of the body and the mind, and were by nature children of wrath, like the rest of mankind. (Eph. 2:1-3)

In every believer's heart, there is a continual battle going on between the flesh and the Spirit (Gal. 5:17). On the plains of battle, footholds are created in our lives from which sin can grow. The language the Bible uses to warn believers of this danger is of a lion stalking its prey. Sin is described as crouching at the door, waiting to devour us (Gen. 4:7). The great news for us, however, is that Jesus is advocating to the Father on our behalf.

My little children, I am writing these things to you so that you may not sin. But if anyone does sin, we have an advocate with the Father, Jesus Christ the righteous. (1 John 2:1)

We see this advocacy in action when Jesus intercedes for Peter, even though Peter will disown Him three times. But note in the verse above that this is the back-up plan. We are commanded not to sin in the first instance. 'That we may not sin'— this is the goal for which every Christian should be striving. With the help of Jesus, we are encouraged not to carry on walking in sin:

Whoever says he abides in him ought to walk in the same way in which he (Jesus) walked. (1 John 2:6)

There is also a clear warning for us that if patterns of sin are persistent, it illuminates that we do not know God (1 John 3:6) and that we ought to question whether the seed of our new life in the Spirit has fallen on fertile soil:

No one born of God makes a practice of sinning, for God's seed abides in him, and he cannot keep on sinning, because he has been born of God. (1 John 3:9)

Knowing the potential of sin to pervade in the life of the believer, we must be about the business of praying for our brothers and sisters in Christ when they fall into sinful patterns.

If anyone sees his brother committing a sin not leading to death, he shall ask, and God will give him life. (1 John 5:16)

This verse raises the alarming reality that there is sin that does lead to death. Rather than being any particular type of sin, the wider biblical picture suggests that repeated sin simply leads to an inability to repent. This is what seems to have happened to Esau:

… that no one is sexually immoral or unholy like Esau, who sold his birthright for a single meal. For you know that afterward, when he desired to inherit the blessing, he was rejected, for he found no chance to repent, though he sought it with tears. (Hebrews 12:16-17)

For this reason, perhaps the most vital Christian practice is to repent and seek forgiveness of sin continually. Any pervading sin in our lives that we are still—by the grace of God—able to repent from is sin that will not lead to death.

If we confess our sins, he is faithful and just to forgive us our sins and to cleanse us from all unrighteousness. (1 John 1:9)

We should, therefore, be immeasurably thankful to God that, despite our ongoing capacity to choose sin, He is merciful to forgive us if we humbly repent. We can also be grateful that the Holy Spirit, given to us as a guarantee (2 Cor. 1:22), helps convict us of sin. The Spirit also brings us into union with Christ. In this union the power of sin is broken—we are able to put off sin and be clothed instead in righteousness.

Remembering that we are both saint and sinner is vital for us. As saints, we remember by God's grace that we've been justified by Jesus. Our inherited position echoes the holy characteristics of Christ, whom we seek to follow.

Although understandably, we may not wish to focus on our position as sinner, there is much to benefit from in keeping this reality in mind. Our potential to fall back into sinful habits should remind us of our daily need for God's mercy, and for the work of the Holy Spirit to convict us of sin. It should also remind us to be realistic about the ongoing fallibility of all Christians and, therefore, to pray continuously for our brothers and sisters who may be struggling with sin.

Finally, how humbling for us to dwell on the truth that, even as we are born into sin, Almighty God still chooses to call us His saints and go about the great work of rendering us fit for redemption.

> Behold what wondrous grace
> The Father hath bestow'd
> On sinners of a mortal race,
> To call them sons of God!
> *(Charles Spurgeon)*

love

'Whoever has my commandments and keeps them, he it
is who loves me.'

John 14:21

obedience

———

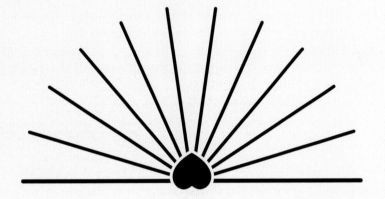

'If you love me, you will keep my commandments.'

love + obedience

A new commandment I give to you, that you love one another: just as I have loved you, you also are to love one another. (John 13:34)

This new commandment has the particular significance of being the last instruction Jesus gives the disciples before going to the cross. It sounds like a reasonably simple directive, and yet, so hard to put into practice. It remains an active command to the church today. But do we really understand what it means 'to love'? And more specifically, do we understand what Jesus meant when He called us to love 'as he loved us'?

If we find this at all confusing, we're in good company. Jesus' command comes immediately after He washes the disciples' feet. Peter is surprised and appalled at this subversion of hierarchy—he cannot believe that the master should wash the servants' feet, and vainly attempts to thwart Jesus' progress.

Peter said to him, 'You shall never wash my feet.' Jesus answered him, 'If I do not wash you, you have no share with me.' (John 13:8)

This exchange reveals something of the difficulty that many of us have in fully accepting God's love: it shouldn't be that the master washes the servants' feet—it shouldn't be that Jesus died in our place. But such is the nature of grace. There's something unexpected—even embarrassing—about being shown this kind of love. Love that is given purely at the cost of the giver—sacrificial love. In the process of washing their feet, Jesus models how this sacrificial love must be given in the least expected circumstances, for the least expected recipients. The disciples would need to apprehend this way of thinking, and put it into practice themselves, as they began the dangerous work of spreading the gospel of grace among the Gentiles.

So how do we align our thinking with Jesus' view of love? I'd like to suggest there are at least two reasons we might grasp the wrong end of the stick on this one. The first is to do with language, the second with culture.

In the Greek language, there are many specific words for different types of love. The main variants are as follows:

- Agape: Sacrificial Love
- Eros: Romantic Love
- Philia: Brotherly Love

- Storge: Familial Love
- Philautia: Self Love

As noted in D.A. Carson's *Exegetical Fallacies*, these translations of the Greek are not always definitive—and sometimes interchangeable. We can, therefore, establish a fairly nuanced picture of the word 'love' in the Bible. Given that our own singular 'four-letter-word' contains the possibility of all these categories, we naturally tend to bring a more direct idea of love to the intended meaning in Scripture. This is then compounded by our cultural emphasis today, which over-stresses the importance of romantic love in particular (what the Greeks would call 'eros' love).

We live in an entertainment-saturated society, which bombards us with the chief aim of fulfilled romantic relationships. So much so, that many people's entire identity is consumed and defined by their 'relationship status'. The nature of the romantic love presented often has no substance—it is to be pursued on a whim, driven by our feelings and can cut across any existing commitment or value. We're told over and over that our individual requirements for happiness and fulfilment through romantic intimacy should trump any obedience to existing marriage vows, family or community responsibilities—any higher commitment at all. It is our primary right to be romantically fulfilled.

It doesn't take long to see the cracks in this mode of thinking. The model is effectively upside-down. Our feelings drive our impulses and actions, and we receive our identity through whatever relationship we land in.

Feelings-Actions-Identity.

Christ, however, calls us instead to put our identity first in Him, to act in obedience to His commandments, and then have our feelings grow out of this position.

Identity-Actions-Feelings.

The implications of this are significant when we consider marriage. How many marriage commitments break down today because people don't 'feel' in love? This is symptomatic of a feelings-first culture. In *Mere Christianity*, C.S. Lewis warned of the fleeting aspect of our feelings:

'Now no feeling can be relied on to last in its full intensity, or even to last at all. Knowledge can last, principles can last, habits can last; but feelings come and go. And in fact, whatever people say, the state called "being in love" usually does not last.'

We should note that the marriage covenant—that we vow our obedience to—doesn't offer us a break clause based on our feelings. On the contrary, they command husband and wife to act in unity—to love and cherish each other—despite the various odds mentioned (for better, for worse, for richer, for poorer, in sickness and in health). It is through being obedient to that commitment, and working at being in love, that feelings of affection consequently grow more deeply. We cherish most what we're most invested in.

And so, through the God-ordained institute of marriage, we see that we must be called through obedience to a sacrificial love that does not come naturally to us—a love that is at odds with the fleeting, selfish, 'feelings-first' love that is prevalent in society.

This primary emphasis on feelings in society also exacerbates confusion over gender and sexuality. Although there is a much broader range of ethical scenarios and experiences than I'm commenting on here, we can at least note briefly how our feelings can distort and confuse the truth in many cases. For example, should someone born as a male 'feel' more feminine in nature, they are entitled to begin a series of actions that will encourage physical change. After this process, they can express their new gender identity in society. Feelings-Actions-Identity. Similarly, if someone is going through adolescence and experiences some moment of same-sex attraction, they are encouraged to act on it and claim this new orientation as their new sexual identity, however fleeting the feelings.

In such cases, prioritising feelings can leave many confused and in great danger of jumping to actions and resolutions that may be irreversible or, at least, grow their affections in a contrary direction. It's important to see that the reverse process is also true.

If we claim our identity first as a child of God—and are obedient to His Word—then our affections grow according to His will. I had the privilege of witnessing a powerful testimony at a New Wine conference, where the speaker shared his struggle with same-sex attraction as a teenager. On coming to faith, he took hold of his identity in Christ, and through obedience to God's commands, his feelings were transformed to a different reality. At the event, he was speaking as a husband and father, and holding to the truth of Paul's command in Scripture:

Do not be conformed to this world, but be transformed by the renewal of your mind, that by testing you may discern what is the will of God, what is good and acceptable and perfect. (Rom. 12:2)

The love that Jesus calls us to display in the world is, of course, not a romantic love, and not a love driven by our emotions. It is 'agape' love—a sacrificial love bound in commitment and obedience. Look at the language used in Scripture to explain how a husband should love his wife:

Husbands, love your wives, as Christ loved the church and gave himself up for her... (Eph. 5:25)

The application of this selfless love is made clear in the covenant of marriage and, not surprisingly, finds its roots in the covenant of grace. As explained more fully in the chapter on 'Blessings + Curses', God's covenant promise helps illuminate the gospel. In so doing, it reveals how God first loved us. Contained within the covenant agreement is this incredible balance of law and love. Jesus poured Himself out for us in sacrificial love, being obedient to the covenant conditions—even unto death.

In the sense that we are partakers of God's covenant, we are committed to loving God in this same selfless way. The nature of this love is identified clearly in John's gospel. When Jesus promises the Holy Spirit to the disciples, He bookends the passage with these two parallel statements:

'If you love me, you will keep my commandments.' (John 14:15) ...
'Whoever has my commandments and keeps them, he it is who loves me.' (John 14:21)

Notice how love and obedience alternate and feed each other in this definitively-formed loop. In this, we get a true sense of the love that we are called to display—a love firmly rooted in obedience. Rather than imagining love and obedience as two separate virtues to uphold, both are brought together in unity to form the kind of incredible, other-centred love that is God.

We see this same integrated relationship of love and obedience required in the church, in our corporate worship of God:

'But the hour is coming, and is now here, when the true worshipers will worship the Father in spirit and truth, for the Father is seeking such people to worship him. God is spirit, and those who worship him must worship in spirit and truth.' (John 4:23–24)

Worshipping in both spirit and truth requires the same blend of love and obedience that we are called to individually. In this, we can see most clearly the pitfalls of including only one side of the equation. A congregation fixed on the Word of God alone, without embracing the transforming work of the Spirit, is as subject to decay as a congregation that purports to be free in the Spirit but neglects to follow Scripture obediently.

In conclusion, love and obedience are both necessary sides of the same coin. They combine to form a love that transcends our natural capacity. It is a love that is evidenced in how God loves us—and it does not come naturally to us. God, in His great wisdom and mercy, has provided us with the necessary help:

'And I will ask the Father, and he will give you another Helper, to be with you for ever, even the Spirit of truth, whom the world cannot receive, because it neither sees him nor knows him. You know him, for he dwells with you and will be in you.' (John 14:16-17)

Our love for each other comes not from our own nature—it is an overflow of God's love in us—the love that we receive by His Spirit, operating both in our lives and in our worship together as His people.

Thanks be to God for the amazing gift of love, given by His Spirit.

Amen.

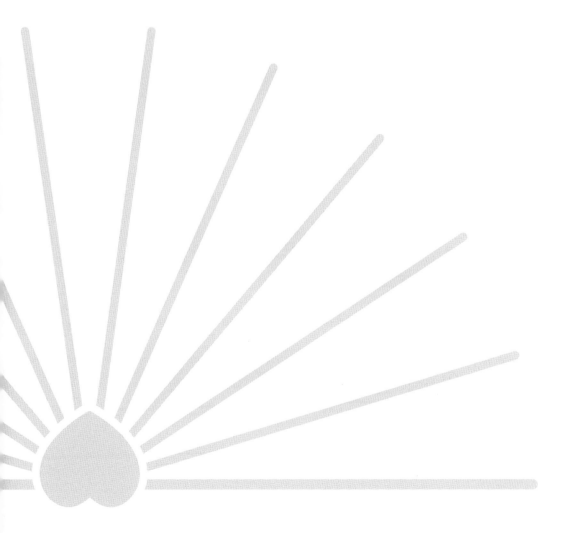

thanks

It would be fair to say that I have more experience with creative solutions than academic theology. To that end, I am incredibly grateful for the many wise heads that took the time to read this work and offer valuable comments. Their patience and insight have helped keep me 'between the lines' and have undoubtedly improved the final outcome.

For their feedback and encouragement, my special thanks to:

Reuben Hunter, Russell Birney, Trevor Morrow, Ivan Steen, David Gray, Harry Smith, Paul Gibson, Paul Fulton, Scott Kelso, my Mum & Dad, and my wife, Emma.

Finally, thanks to editor John van Eyk and Christian Focus Publications for their faithfulness and expertise in bringing this project to fruition.

To Biba, Oban & Thea, for legacy

details

About the Author

—

Ross Cunningham studied Architecture at Nottingham University and has worked in the creative industry for over twenty years. He has worked primarily in London and across the UK, Russia and the Middle East. Ross recently returned to his native Northern Ireland with wife Emma and their three children. The family attends Belfast City Vineyard, where Ross serves as part of the leadership team.

Notes

—

Unless otherwise stated, the English Standard Version of the Bible 'ESVUK' has been used throughout. Copyright © Crossway Bibles. Scripture marked 'MSG' is taken from The Message. Copyright © 1993, 1994, 1995, 1996, 2000, 2001, 2002. Used by permission of NavPress Publishing Group. Scripture marked 'NIV' is taken from the Holy Bible, New International Version®, NIV® Copyright © 1973, 1978, 1984, 2011 by Biblica, Inc.™ Used by permission. All rights reserved worldwide. Scripture quotations marked 'NLT' are taken from the Holy Bible, New Living Translation, copyright © 1996. Used by permission of Tyndale House Publishers, Inc., Wheaton, Illinois 60189. All rights reserved.

Publishing details

—

ISBN 978-1-5271-0637-6
First published in 2021
Christian Focus Publications Ltd,
Geanies House, Fearn, Ross-shire, IV20 1TW, Scotland, UK
www.christianfocus.com

Design details

—

Printed by Gutenberg, Malta
Cover design and illustrations by Ross Cunningham
All text and images copyright © Ross Cunningham 2021
www.rosscunningham.com
www.bothand.org.uk

All rights reserved

—

CHRISTIAN FOCUS PUBLICATIONS

Christian Focus Publications Ltd,
Geanies House, Fearn, Ross-shire,
IV20 1TW, Scotland, United Kingdom.
www.christianfocus.com

OUR MISSION STATEMENT:

— *Staying Faithful* —

In dependence upon God we seek to impact the world through literature faithful to His infallible Word, the Bible. Our aim is to ensure that the Lord Jesus Christ is presented as the only hope to obtain forgiveness of sin, live a useful life and look forward to heaven with Him.

—

Our books are published in four imprints:

CHRISTIAN FOCUS

Popular works including biographies, commentaries, basic doctrine and Christian living.

CHRISTIAN HERITAGE

Books representing some of the best material from the rich heritage of the church.

MENTOR

Books written at a level suitable for Bible College and seminary students, pastors, and other serious readers. The imprint includes commentaries, doctrinal studies, examination of current issues and church history.

CF4•K

Children's books for quality Bible teaching and for all age groups: Sunday school curriculum, puzzle and activity books; personal and family devotional titles, biographies and inspirational stories — because you are never too young to know Jesus!